Unconquered People

Native Peoples, Cultures, and Places of the Southeastern United States

Native Peoples, Cultures, and Places of the Southeastern United States
Jerald T. Milanich, Series Editor

Each volume in this series is intended to provide a highly readable overview of an American Indian group, the culture of a discrete period, region or place, a major archaeological site, or a specific topic of interest crossing many cultures. The goal is to make readers aware of the Native American heritage of the southeastern United States.

The Apalachee Indians and Mission San Luis by John H. Hann and Bonnie G. McEwan (1998)
Florida's Indians from Ancient Times to the Present by Jerald T. Milanich (1998)
Unconquered People: Florida's Seminole and Miccosukee Indians by Brent Richards Weisman (1999)
The Ancient Mounds of Poverty Point: Place of Rings, by Jon L. Gibson (2000)
Before and After Jamestown: Virginia's Powhatans and Their Predecessors, by Helen C. Rountree and E. Randolph Turner (2002); first paperback edition, 2005
Ancient Miamians: The Tequesta of South Florida, by William E. McGoun (2002)
The Archaeology and History of the Native Georgia Tribes, by Max E. White (2002)
The Calusa and Their Legacy: South Florida People and Their Environments, by Darcie A. MacMahon and William H. Marquardt (2004)

→ Unconquered People ←

Florida's Seminole and
Miccosukee Indians

↑ ↑ ↑ ↑ ↑ ↑ ↑ ↑ ↑ ↑ ↑ ↑ ↑

Brent Richards Weisman

University Press of Florida
Gainesville · Tallahassee · Tampa · Boca Raton
Pensacola · Orlando · Miami · Jacksonville

Title page drawing by Theodore Morris
Cover art by Mary Gay Osceola

09 08 07 06 05 04   6 5 4 3 2

Library of Congress Cataloging-in-Publication Data
Weisman, Brent Richards, 1952–
Unconquered people: Florida's Seminole and Miccosukee Indians /
Brent Richards Weisman.
p. cm. — (Native peoples, cultures, and places
of the southeastern United States)
Includes bibliographical references
ISBN 0-8130-1662-2 (cloth: alk. paper)
ISBN 0-8130-1663-0 (pbk.)
1. Seminole Indians—History. 2. Seminole Indians—Social life and
customs. 3. Mikasuki Indians—History. 4. Mikasuki Indians—Social
life and customs. I. Title. II. Series.
E99.S28 W434 1999
975.9'00493—dc21 98-30329

The University Press of Florida is the scholarly publishing agency for
the State University System of Florida, comprising Florida A&M
University, Florida Atlantic University, Florida International
University, Florida State University, University of Central Florida,
University of Florida, University of North Florida, University of
South Florida, and University of West Florida.

University Press of Florida
15 Northwest 15th Street
Gainesville, FL 32611
http://www.upf.com

CONTENTS

FOREWORD

Ask who the Seminole Indians are and most people would correctly identify them as Native Americans living in Florida. Many fewer would know that significant numbers of Seminole Indians also live in Oklahoma or that individuals of Seminole ancestry, like other Americans, reside in small towns and large urban centers from New York City to the Bay Area in California. Even fewer would be aware of the history of the Seminoles, who once lived in isolation in southern Florida but today run a sophisticated and instructional page on the World Wide Web and maintain their equally educational museum.

In this popularly written and well-illustrated volume, anthropologist Brent Weisman brings fresh perspectives to the Seminoles, explaining how they emerged as an ethnic group during the colonial period. He also relates that history to the rich legacy of the precolumbian Indians of the southeastern United States. Weisman, a friend to the Seminoles as well as a scholar of their culture, leads us through the eighteenth and nineteenth centuries to the present, weaving together the historical and archaeological sources that allow us to understand the changes that took place in Seminole lifeways even while these resilient people retained the core of their identity and heritage. Past and present, traditional and new—all blend together in the modern Seminole and Miccosukee Indians.

Miccosukee Indians? Who are they? As Weisman explains, the Miccosukee, another modern-day South Florida tribe, share a history and close ties to the Seminoles. It was the politics of the mid-twentieth century that resulted in the formation of two separate federally recognized groups, the Seminole Tribe of Florida and the Miccosukee Tribe.

In a concluding chapter that readers will find especially refreshing, Weisman provides an annotated atlas of the sites and places they can visit to learn more about these Florida Indians whose fascinating history lies all across the Florida landscape. This practical guide brings us face to face with aspects of the cultures of the Seminole and Miccosukee, an exercise that creates a unique portrait of their shared lifeways through time. Brent Weisman and the people he writes about, the Seminole and Miccosukee Indians, are to be congratulated on this excellent addition to our series, Native Peoples, Cultures, and Places of the Southeastern United States.

Jerald T. Milanich
SERIES EDITOR

ACKNOWLEDGMENTS

There are many people to thank for their help in putting this book together, first to Jerald Milanich, editor of the Native Peoples series at the University Press of Florida, for the invitation to contribute this volume to the series. Jerry's comments, those of the editorial staff at the press, and suggestions made by two anonymous reviewers all greatly strengthened the manuscript.

John Ehrenhard of the National Park Service and Steve Martin, Pat Wells, Barbara Roberts, Jack Gillen, and Howard Adams of the Florida Park Service generously provided photographs and other information from their files. Robert S. Carr of the Archaeological and Historical Conservancy allowed me to reproduce photographs from several important projects in South Florida. Harry and Jackie Piper read portions of the manuscript concerning the Fort Brooke cemetery and graciously allowed me to reprint photographs from their earlier publications. At the University of South Florida, Ted Fassler helped prepare the maps that appear in chapter 8, and Keith Ryder helped compile information about several sites described in that chapter.

I am grateful to artists Ted Morris and Mary Gay Osceola for letting their creative works appear on these pages. Eric von Schmidt deserves mention for his artistic interest in the project, and may our paths cross on the next one. Billy Cypress, Mary Gay Osceola, and Patsy West indulged my questions about specific aspects of Seminole culture and history. William Sturtevant provided information about Seminole collections held at the Smithsonian Institution. Viviene Gooden provided current information about the Willoughby Collection at the Elliott Museum in Stuart. Paula

Willey of the American Museum of Natural History and Martha Labell of the Harvard Peabody Museum of Archaeology and Ethnology greatly facilitated access to photographs under their care. And thanks to my daughter Rachel for her good spirit and sense of adventure on the Seminole trail in the wilds of South Florida.

Introduction

Who are the Seminoles? Where did they come from? Why did their culture survive when many other American Indian cultures lost their identity? The purpose of this book is to try to provide answers to these and other common and most intriguing questions concerning the history and culture of the Florida Seminole Indians. Never before has it been more important to appreciate the role of the Seminoles in shaping the Florida of today. Many of Florida's citizens know of the Seminoles only what they read in the newspaper, not all of it favorable, mostly reporting the latest controversy regarding gaming, disputed land and water rights taken to court, or tribal business deals given an extra measure of legislative or judicial scrutiny. Few know that the more than twenty-six hundred contemporary Seminoles and Micosukees, are descended from fewer than two hundred survivors left at the end of the last Seminole war in 1858. Few know that the historical Seminole are divided into two federally recognized nations, the Seminole Tribe of Florida, recognized in 1957, and the Miccosukee Tribe of Indians of Florida, chartered in 1962 [hereafter, except when referring specifically to the Miccosukee Tribe as a political entity, the word *Seminole* will be used to cover the cultural developments of both modern tribes]. Two distinct southeastern Indian languages are spoken among them: Mikasuki by the Miccosukee and most of the Seminoles, and Muskogee by the Seminoles of the Brighton Reservation. It is little known that the Seminoles run a multi-million-dollar cattle enterprise and one of the most profitable lemon and citrus packing houses in the state. For several years during the early 1980s, Seminole contributions to statewide political campaigns ranked among the largest of the corporate donors, earning them political capital far beyond their small numbers. Today's Seminoles and Miccosukees have stepped out from the shadows of the past. Now it is time for the story of their history and culture to come out into the sunshine.

This is a book about the culture and history of the Florida Seminoles, but it is not *their* story. It is not truly possible, much less even remotely desirable, for any anthropologist or historian to speak for the Seminoles. They tell their own stories and speak with their own voices. But what the scholar can hope to do, what I hope to do here, is to weave together strands from multiple lines of evidence, each contributing to the overall strength and beauty of the fabric. I will bring together six lines of evidence to build the fabric of this narrative. That there is so much to work with means that Seminole scholarship has come of age.

Anthropologists tell us a great many things about Seminole culture and bring a comparative approach that places the emergence and development of Seminole culture within the broader framework of Creek Indian traditions and other American Indian cultures. Such a perspective is essential in understanding what is uniquely Seminole and how Seminole culture was able to transform age-old customs and beliefs into living traditions valued by modern people. Three anthropologists in particular managed to advance our knowledge of the Seminoles through firsthand observation, despite the justifiable reluctance on the part of the natives to submit to such observation. These scholars are Alexander Spoehr, Louis Capron (by profession a dentist), and William Sturtevant, whose works form an important foundation for this book.

Historians, whose primary focus is on the political, economic, and military relationships between the Seminoles and the dominant white society, tell us much about how the identities of both groups were mutually defined by the experience. James Covington and J. Leitch Wright covered a broad range of historical issues, while John Mahon evaluated the tragedy of the Seminole wars as a clash of cultures with very different concepts of the methods and objectives of warfare. The complex modern era of federal tribal recognition, reservation politics, and the land claims cases against the U.S. government has been examined by historian Harry Kersey, certainly one of the few scholars to grasp the intricacies of the current situation.

Archaeologists like myself find many challenges in unraveling the Seminole past, and our work comprises a third source of knowledge about Seminole culture. One striking observation is the abundance of European-derived trade goods that mark Seminole sites of the late 1700s and early 1800s. Does this indicate their success as businessmen on the colonial Florida frontier? Archaeology also is very good at demonstrating the former range of the Seminoles, once spread throughout the panhandle and peninsula. In areas that many contemporary Floridians call home—subdivisions of east Gainesville, the quiet lanes and orange groves of Inverness, the urban sprawl of Tampa and Dade and Broward counties—Seminoles of previous centuries hunted, fished, grew crops of corn, pumpkins, even rice, and herded cattle. Like the panther, their restricted distribution in modern times reflects a response to the expansion of a hostile, aggressive society rather than a deliberate choice to live in less-than-favorable circumstances.

John Goggin and Charles Fairbanks during their years at the University of Florida made pioneering contributions to Seminole archaeology with their studies of Seminole artifacts and in their use of historical sources to identify and interpret the Seminole archaeological record. Seminole archaeology is now more active than ever, with new finds being reported yearly from South Florida and other locations now within reach of the survey archaeologist. Preservation of Seminole Indian archaeological sites also is enjoying high priority as the State of Florida, through its Conservation and Recreation Lands (CARL) acquisition program, recently paid nearly $2 million for the fifty-three-acre Snake Warrior site in Broward County and more than $3.5 million for the ninety-nine-acre Pine Island Ridge site in that same county. These sites, both important in the nineteenth-century settlement of South Florida by the Seminoles, will be preserved as public parks.

Another way in which we can learn about the Seminoles is by looking at the ways in which their distinctive clothing, jewelry, crafts, and other objects of material culture changed through time. Combining anthropology, history, and an appreciation of folk arts, Dorothy Downs, David Blackard, and Patsy West are carrying forward in areas first explored by Goggin and Sturtevant. Many people are interested to learn that patchwork, the single trait most often associated with the Seminoles by the general public, did not come into its own as a decorative style until the sewing machine became available in the early years of the twentieth century.

Another source of information is provided by the narratives of early travelers, government agents, sportsmen, journalists, and various others whose activities brought them into contact with the Seminoles during different periods of their history. Eclectic, uneven, often biased and judgmental, these accounts nonetheless reward the reader with details of geography, individual behavior and idioms, and behind-the-scenes intrigues absent from strictly anthropological or historical studies. Perhaps there is no better introduction to Seminole culture and its changes than a comparison of William Bartram's 1770s account of Seminole life at Cuscowilla near the Alachua savanna and Clay MacCauley's report on the isolated camps of the Okeechobee area written one hundred years later. Sometime between the log houses of Bartram and the chickees of MacCauley, between the squareground of Cuscowilla and the dance ground in the pine barrens of South Florida, emerges the unique Seminole identity.

Finally, of growing importance, we have the voices of the Seminoles themselves. In stories, songs, and oral histories, Betty Mae Jumper, David Jumper, James Billie, Mary Frances Johns, and others bring Seminole history and culture both to a younger generation of Seminoles and to a Florida public eager for the authentic. The best sources of information about contemporary Seminole life are the Seminole and Miccosukee tribal newspapers. The *Seminole Tribune* regularly scoops the more mainstream papers in the state on the latest issues regarding Indian affairs, often with more complete and detailed coverage. The paper is quick to champion the rights of the underdog, especially if the state or federal government was responsible for the wrongdoing. The James Billie panther trial, the much-delayed Seminole land claims settlement, and the award of compensation for the notorious Rosewood incident all received their fullest, and arguably best, treatment in the Seminole paper.

Seminole studies are not relegated to the past. The Seminoles are not an extinct culture, known only through the dry dust of archaeology or the yellowed pages of history. Far from it. Theirs is a living history. Although deeply rooted in the remote past of southeastern prehistory, the Seminoles of today are very much a product of the modern era. No full account of the Seminole people can favor past over present, or vice versa. The view presented in these pages is of Seminole culture as a fusion of both.

1

Becoming Seminole

✦ ✦ ✦ ✦ ✦ ✦ ✦ ✦ ✦ ✦ ✦ ✦

The Seminoles are a hard people to get to know. Part of this is their own doing. Their reluctance to talk about their culture is legendary among anthropologists. True, Josie Billy did talk to anthropologist William Sturtevant in the 1950s, but by all accounts Josie Billy was a very unusual Seminole. Because he would discuss Seminole customs and traditions in great detail, sometimes with little prompting, Josie Billie was considered by Sturtevant to be the only Seminole worth talking to. Most gave the anthropologist the cold shoulder, answering "I don't know" to his simplest questions. Other anthropologists met with even less success. A young graduate student from Yale abandoned her attempt at fieldwork among the Tamiami Trail groups in 1944 when she was linked to some spurious intrigue invented by Indians who did not want her there. Anthropologists and Seminoles have not done well together. As a result, the Seminoles have not entered the mainstream of anthropological attention and are poorly known to those who know well the cultures of the Hopi and Navajo.

The history of the Seminoles adds another element of mystery. Documentary accounts before the third quarter of the 1700s do not call the Indians then living in Florida "Seminole." Lower Creeks, Yuchis, even Yamasees were reported to be roaming the Florida frontier, depending on the observer's vantage point, but rarely, "Seminoles." Even in the 1800s during the infamous Seminole wars, chroniclers were more likely to write about bands of Tallasees, Mikasukis (various spellings), Tohopekaligas, or simply the "enemy," rather than the blanket term *Seminole.* When did the Seminoles, as such, become a political nation? The Indian Claims Commission of the U.S. Justice Department wanted to know. The stakes were high. Some $12 million in land claims settlements hung in the balance. The best and the brightest in Seminole scholarship were brought forward to present their findings in hearings held in the 1950s. The research, voluminous as it was, only weakly supported the conclusion that by the early

1800s the Florida Indians were operating independently of their Creek relatives and had some degree of political autonomy under the rubric Seminole.

Left unresolved was the important question of the historical basis for the split between the Seminoles and Miccosukees, culturally and historically intertwined but each with its own federally recognized tribe. What lands could each tribe claim? What compensation was rightly due? History was of no help in these decisions, because history has not been good at recording those things most important to the Indians.

Neither has archaeology done much to illuminate the mysteries of the Seminole past. They have traveled lightly over the earth. No monumental temples or tombs stand as witness to their past cultural achievements, although we know that Seminole rituals and religion were complex. Circular clearings of bare packed earth and ashes from the busk fire are all that mark their ceremonial grounds. Their ancient villages and towns contain no collapsed stone walls, no roofless empty rooms. Burned chickee posts and scattered sherds of broken glass are the most that remain. Often the evidence is far less. Although Seminole towns once overlooked Lake Miccosukee in the Tallahassee Red Hills, the banks of the Suwannee and St. Johns rivers, the prairie of the Alachua savanna, and the lakes of Central Florida, all but the most astute observer would miss the most tangible marker of former Seminole presence, pottery sherds with a brushed surface in the typical Seminole style. Brushed pottery is important for another reason. It is the simplest and most common aspect of material culture linking the early Seminoles to their Creek ancestry, and through it, to their ultimate roots deep in southeastern prehistory. Before there were Seminoles there were Creeks, and before there were Creeks there were the mound-building chiefdoms of the broad floodplains and river valleys of the interior Southeast.

The Ancestral Creek Tradition

Pushing the Seminole story back in time one goes from the transformation of Creek to Seminole and from pre-Creek to Creek. Geographically we must move northward from Florida to the rolling country of middle Georgia and Alabama (fig. 1.1). In this backward journey one must be careful about applying the term *Creek* to the peoples of late prehistory, since the word originated with English use in the eighteenth century and was their reference to the groups with whom they were trading on the creeks of the Georgia and Alabama piedmont. Archaeologists long have recognized that

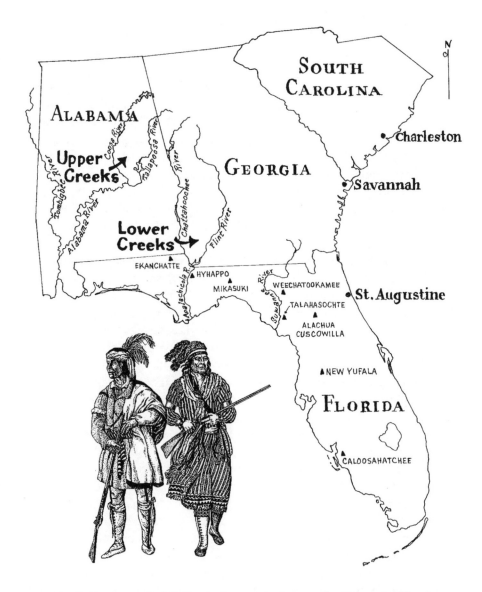

1.1. Creek Country and early Seminole towns prior to 1783. (Drawn by Theodore Morris, reproduced with the artist's permission.)

a fundamental continuity of traits archaeologically measurable connects the historic-period Creeks with the prehistoric mound builders of Georgia and Alabama. Looking to the archaeological record, they have sought the origins of Creek chiefdom-level society and the Green Corn Dance or busk practices known from historical observations.

Archaeologists look at fire pits or hearths in the individual layers of earthen fill that together make a temple or platform mound and see evidence of the periodic purification rituals that underlie the busk ceremony of the historic period. Conch shell cups and dippers buried in the mounds suggest that the black drink ritual, a core part of the Green Corn ceremony, has considerable time depth back into prehistory. The facts that these ceremonial mounds were used for many hundreds of years and grew larger through time with the addition of fresh layers of fill suggest the existence of chiefdoms, and chiefdoms, by definition, mean that leadership, power, and control were determined on the basis of kinship. Kinship organization of these late prehistoric societies most likely would have been divided according to clan, with membership determined by relationship to female ancestors as was true of the matrilineal clans of the historic period. Thus it is possible to trace backward through time the essential features of Creek Indian culture known to historic observers and see Creek cultural development as a logical consequence of local or regional interactions between culture and environment.

Although archaeological studies indicate that the large mound centers of late prehistory were built by societies whose ancestors had been in the Southeast for many thousands of years, perhaps back to Paleoindian times about 12,000 years ago, the migration legend of the Creeks tells a different tale. In the version recounted to Georgia governor James Oglethorpe by Chiscaliche, the "Cherokee-Killer," in the mid-1700s, the Creeks cast themselves in the role of invaders, fighting adversity on their push east into their new territory. William Bartram carried this idea even further when he wrote that Oconee Creeks under the leadership of Ahaya, or Cowkeeper, had intentionally relocated their town from Central Georgia to the rim of the Alachua savanna in Central Florida, in the midst of a peninsula inhabited by Tomocos, Utinas, Calloosas, Yamases (all in Bartram's spelling), and other remnant tribes driven south by the Carolina British, all of whom were hostile to the Creek newcomers.

Aided by Spaniards from St. Augustine, these groups repeatedly attacked the Oconee town at Cuscowilla until finally the Oconees were strengthened by arrivals from their "uncles" the Upper Creeks, and the tables were turned. Not only did the Creeks vanquish their Indian enemies, said Bartram, but they also fell on and destroyed the Spanish settlements, which we can presume to mean isolated cattle ranchos and missions of Central and North Florida. Because Bartram made the town of Cuscowilla important to this story, we know that he was referring to Cowkeeper's early years in Florida, in the poorly known time between about 1740 and 1763, but mostly Bartram's account is difficult to square with historical fact. He seems to have combined elements of at least two separate historical events: the attacks on the Timucua and Apalachee missions by British-backed Creeks and Yamasees in the late seventeenth and early eighteenth centuries, and the Creek use of the Florida peninsula as far south as the Everglades for hunting grounds during this same period. True or not, Bartram's tale reinforces the Creeks' own notion that their history represents a cultural wedge driven into the aboriginal Southeast. The movement into Florida was but the latest push of the wedge, a push resulting in the birth of the Seminoles.

Combining archaeological evidence, the written observations of the early chroniclers, and the oral traditions of the Indians themselves, we can reconstruct what might be called the ancestral Creek pattern. This was the base from which Seminole Indian culture developed. We can understand the ancestral Creek pattern as containing the following elements.

Society was organized into matrilineal clans, some named after animals (Panther, Bear, Deer), others after natural forces (Wind), and others after plants (Potato or Corn). Clan membership was determined through the mother's line and was traced back to a common female ancestor. A man was a member of his mother's clan, yet his children were members of his wife's (their mother's) clan. Through a set of responsibilities a man was forever tied to his mother's residence and had a strong relationship with his sister's children, who were members of his clan. The clans were organized into two groups or moieties, red and white, the colors of war and peace. Although Red and White clans coexisted in each town, the town itself carried a designation as either Red or White. At the level of town government, decisions regarding peacetime activities were made by the White clans, at times of war by the Red. When external circumstances required cooperative decisions on the part of two or more towns, Red towns took the lead in war and White during times of peace. Red towns played White towns in the ball game, the "little brother of war," a rollicking free-for-all often lasting weeks and involving much injury and large wagers on the outcome. The early Seminole towns in Florida maintained this formal relationship through the 1770s and were observed on several occasions during this and the previous decade making "little war" on each other.

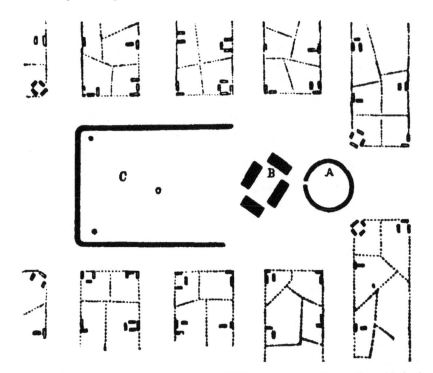

1.2. A Creek squareground, 1789, drawn by William Bartram. (Originally published in 1853 in the *Transactions of the American Ethnological Society*, vol. 3.) *A* is the rotunda, *B* the squareground, *C* the chunky yard. Also shown are the household compounds surrounding the squareground.

Central to each town was the squareground (fig. 1.2, *B*), the local seat of government, where people would gather for councils, to welcome visitors, or to celebrate the annual busk. In the center of the square was the council fire with its four logs pointing to the cardinal directions. Bounding the square were four cabins, each with two or more rows of benches facing the square. In the west cabin were seated men from the White clans. Men from the Red clans sat in the north cabin. Their assistants and the chief's advisors sat together in the south cabin, and women and children sat to the east. Adjacent to one corner of the square was the "round house," sometimes as large as one hundred feet in diameter and fifty feet tall, where winter councils were held. The squareground was kept scrupulously clean. Before the annual busk ceremony, the dirt from the surface of the squareground was swept away to form low ridges surrounding the square behind the benches or was heaped to create a low mound off to one side. Some anthropologists view this process as a downscaled version of the ceremonial mound-building practices of prehistoric Mississippian societies of the interior Southeast and thus see evidence of cultural continuity between the Creeks and earlier prehistoric Indian societies.

Despite the political importance of the towns, most of the people lived outside them, spread along the banks of the rivers and streams in smaller household settlements called *huti,* or clan camps. Although tied to its town by bonds of politics and ceremony, the camp for the most part was self-sufficient, producing what it needed to survive from agricultural fields and gardens and taking care of its own needs. The matrilineal focus of the camp and the strength of the kinship bond ensured that married sons who lived elsewhere could be called upon if needed. Archaeologists recognize these settlements in the late prehistoric archaeological record as discrete concentrations of broken pottery, stone tools, dark, midden-stained earth, storage or refuse pits, and clusters of postholes belonging to closely associated buildings. The clan camp was the most stable, unchanging form of settlement in the aboriginal Southeast, persisting among the Seminoles of South Florida well into the twentieth century, long after they stopped living in squareground towns.

Religion of the ancestral Creeks was based on the concepts of purity and balance, concerns that, again, can be traced archaeologically to their mound-building predecessors. Purity was achieved by fasting, drinking the black drink, scratching or bleeding, bathing, and other ritual means in the opening days of the Green Corn Dance or busk, while balance and harmony were sought on the final day through the airing of grievances and wrongdoing.

Diversity in the Creek Tradition

Recognizing this pattern of traits helps unify our understanding of the Creek cultural foundation from which the Seminoles developed. But in our haste to generalize we must not ignore the fact that significant diversity existed among the many Creek bands. Specific differences in historical origin aside, only rarely did the Creek bands ally themselves into a confederacy for political action. The so-called Creek Confederacy that long has fascinated anthropologists was most likely a response to historical circumstances, not an indigenous form of government. Chroniclers of the de Soto expedition fail to provide strong evidence for the existence of a confederation among the pre-Creeks of the 1540s. Beyond that, there are the questions of how frequently and for what purposes the historic Creek towns did pull together for unified political action. Ultimately, it is not possible to understand the development of the Creek Confederacy and its influence without taking into account the political skills and motivations of the "Emperor" Brim of Coweta in the opening decades of the 1700s and Alexander MacGillivray later in the century.

Indeed, Brim's actions as mastermind of the Yamasee War inadvertently set the stage for the first sustained movement of Creek towns into Florida. The failed assault by the Yamasee on British South Carolina meant failure for the rest of Brim's unified attack on the British and Spanish colonists, and his Lower Creeks moved deeper into the interior as a protection against any attempted retaliatory strikes. In their towns along the Chattahoochee River, these Lower Creeks were nicely positioned to move into Florida, then largely vacant due to the destruction and collapse of the Spanish missions.

At this point the cultural geography of the Creek colonial frontier takes on sharper definition. Differences between towns in terms of language, geographical location, and pro-British or pro-Spanish sympathies (if, indeed, any pronounced sympathy existed) become important to understand because of their consequences for the early history and development of the Seminoles. First is the distinction between the Upper and Lower Creeks. The extent to which this division existed prior to the early European presence in the Southeast is open for speculation, but British colonial expansion into interior Georgia after 1670 clearly stimulated the separate development of these two groups.

To the east, along the Ocmulgee and Chattahoochee rivers and at points in between, were the Lower Creeks. Their position on the colonial frontier made them the first point of contact for both British and Spanish traders or envoys; thus they quickly learned what motivated the colonists and became skilled in maintaining their own interests. It was from the Lower Creeks that the founding populations of Seminoles were to come; indeed Lower Creek settlements existed in Florida's Apalachicola Valley before sustained Lower Creek settlement occurred in the Tallahassee or Alachua savanna areas. Through the 1760s and 1770s, the terms *Lower Creek* and *Seminole* (or derivatives of them) were often used interchangeably by writers in referring to the new Florida towns.

The Upper Creeks were centered on the Tallapoosa and Coosa river drainages of Central Alabama, more remote from the seats of British and Spanish colonial authority on the Atlantic seaboard and buffered in that contact by the Lower Creeks. For their part, the Upper Creeks were the first line of contact with the French colony at Mobile and had little directly to do with the British. It was not until after the American Revolution that white presence became a regular feature of Upper Creek life, and this by American pioneers wanting Creek land. Thus began the tensions between Creek factions and between the Creeks and Americans that would culminate in the Creek War of 1813–1814. As we will see in chapter 3, the devastation of the Upper Creeks as the result of that war sent many refugees as a second wave of migration into Florida, where they would assume new identities as Seminoles.

Politics was not the only thing separating the Creeks. A major difference was in language; two distinct and mutually unintelligible Muskhogean languages were spoken in Creek country, not to mention individual towns in which Koasati, Shawnee, Alabama, or Yuchi tongues dominated. In many Creek towns Muskogee was spoken, and this was the common language used for communication between towns or at the level of the confederacy. However, a sizeable minority of Creek towns, particularly among the Lower Creeks, spoke Hitchiti, sometimes referred to in contemporary accounts as the Stinkard tongue, based obviously on the perspectives of nonspeakers.

Like their Creek ancestors, today's Seminole and Miccosukee Indians speak two languages, a fact not recognized by whites until early in the twentieth century, and a fact that still surprises many people. Muskogee, or "Creek" as it is sometimes called, is still spoken by the Seminoles of Brighton Reservation and Fort Pierce, whose ancestry can be easily traced to the Central Florida bands led by Tallahassee and Chipco. To Muskogee speakers, the word for Indian or "red person" is *istica ti. Sofkee*, derived from the Muskogee word for corn soup, and *coontie*, from the Muskogee word for the starchy *Zamia* plant from which the Seminoles processed flour, are words recognizable to many English speakers in Florida. Despite the dominance of Muskogee among the Creeks, most Seminoles and Miccosukees speak the Mikasuki language, a dialect of the extinct Hitchiti. Mikasuki speakers in Florida in the late 1800s and early 1900s used Muskogee in their dealings with the outside world, just as the Creeks had used this language as a lingua franca in Creek country.

From Creek to Seminole

By 1716 the Spanish colonial government in St. Augustine was sending agents to the Lower Creeks in an attempt to entice them to resettle in the abandoned mission fields of North Florida. Spanish timing was perfect: the Lower Creeks were still on the move following their failed attempt to drive the British out of Carolina in the Yamasee War. Over the next several decades the towns of Apalachicola, Oconee, Yuchi, and Sawokli moved into the former Apalachee province. By royal decree, the Spanish established a trading post at St. Marks in 1745, a further attempt to stabilize Lower Creek settlement in North Florida. When the Lower Creeks responded by bringing in more deerskins than the post could handle, the weakness of Spain's Indian policy was exposed. Now there was cause for disenchantment with both the British and Spanish colonial governments.

As the Lower Creeks in Florida moved further away from the Creek sphere of influence they began to take on an identity as "Seminoles," *cimarrones* or wild ones, on the margins of the Creek heartland. This new identity was further reinforced by the attitude of wariness adopted by the Florida towns regarding the colonial authorities. If the birth of the Seminole can be traced to a specific time and place, that date is November 18, 1765, the place, Picolata on the banks of the St. Johns River west of St. Augustine. Florida was now under British rule, and here, under a thatched-roof pavilion built for the occasion, fifty Lower Creek chiefs gathered to hear Governor Grant's request for the concession of lands east of the St. Johns. Grant considered the Lower Creeks the proper audience for his request and flatly stated that the entire peninsula was under their control.

Before getting down to business, Grant and the Indian superintendent John Stuart watched from the pavilion as the Creeks performed the Calumet, or Pipe of Peace, Ceremony. The Indians moved toward them in two columns. At the front of one column six Creeks carried twenty dressed buckskins, at the head of the other walked two chiefs, carrying the calumet pipe decorated with eagle feathers. With a halting pace, singing, shouting, and dancing, the Indians advanced, until finally only the chiefs with the pipe moved up to stroke Grant and Stuart with the eagle feathers. The deerskins were then presented, and the pipe of peace was lighted and smoked by the two Englishmen and the chiefs. What Grant did not understand was that Cowkeeper of the Alachua band held himself apart from this conference, and in so doing made it clear that the Lower Creeks did not speak for his interest. When Cowkeeper took time out from hunting to travel to St. Augustine in December with his retinue of sixty to meet personally with Grant on his own terms, exclusive Creek control over the peninsula was effectively broken. Cowkeeper returned home a "Great Medal Chief." After this, travelers, traders, and government officials increasingly referred to the Indians of North and Central Florida as Seminoles.

Cowkeeper, in Grant's estimation one of the most intelligent Indians on the scene, quickly became the central figure in the emergence of the Seminole nation and exerted a strong influence over events in Seminole country

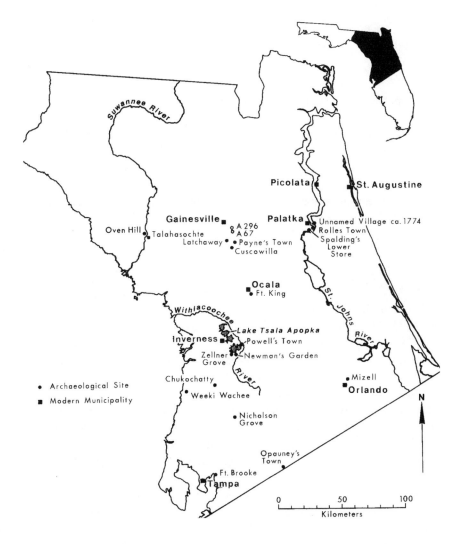

1.3. Locations of Seminole archaeological and historical sites in North Florida.

for some thirty years. The Alachua savanna south of present-day Gainesville (today's Paynes Prairie) (fig. 1.3) would thus become a heartland of the Seminole nation, a geographical center to which many later Seminoles—Payne, Micanopy, and Bowlegs among them—could trace their roots. Despite this importance, Cowkeeper's early towns of Lachua, on the rim of the vast Paynes Prairie, and Cuscowilla, on the trading path several miles distant, remain archaeologically undiscovered. Cowkeeper himself can only be glimpsed in the known documents of the period, perhaps reflecting his desire and ability to keep his distance from the colonial authorities.

William Bartram Meets the Seminoles

One who had the opportunity to see Cowkeeper and his Seminoles close up left a remarkably eloquent account of those experiences. This was William Bartram, the Quaker naturalist born in 1739 on the banks of the Schuylkill River in Philadelphia, son of the noted botanist John Bartram. Early demonstrating a remarkable skill of his own for botany and sketching from nature, William was able to win a place on his father's botanical expedition to Florida commissioned by George III in 1765, just in time to witness the dramatic calumet ceremony at Picolata. The study of the southeastern Indians was thus added to the young Bartram's passion for observation. After repeated failings as a businessman and planter, in April 1773 William Bartram again found himself part of an expedition to Florida. This one was in fact at his own instigation, one senses, as a last ditch effort to make something of himself in practical terms. Bartram managed to convince Dr. John Fothergill to front his venture, which consisted of collecting seeds and plants for a prospective horticultural business in Europe. Fothergill encouraged Bartram to confine his collecting to areas of the Southeast most like Europe, such as the Upper Piedmont and Appalachians, but Bartram felt no obligation to do so. His interest was in ranging as broadly as opportunity would allow, and he wasted no time in making his way up the St. Johns River past Picolata and then overland west into the heart of Seminole country. Ultimately his journey lasted more than three years and took him to see the Cherokees deep in what is now North Carolina, the Upper Creeks of the Coosa and Tallapoosa rivers, and as far west as Spanish Louisiana. His *Travels*, published in 1791, riveted the attention of intellectuals, poets, and naturalists on the American Southeast and is today considered a classic of American literature and an extraordinary primary source on the southeastern Indians. Few people encountered by Bartram during his travels impressed him as much as Cowkeeper, and some of his keenest prose is directed to Cowkeeper and his Cuscowilla band.

Bartram recounts his meeting with Cowkeeper in April 1774 this way:

> We arrived at Cuscowilla, near the banks: a pretty brook of water ran through the town, and entered the lake just by. We were welcomed to the town, and conducted by the young men and maidens to the chief's

house, which stood on an eminence, and was distinguished from the rest by its superior magnitude, a large flag being hoisted on a high staff at one corner. We immediately alighted: the chief, who is called the Cowkeeper, attended by several ancient men, came to us, and in a very free and sociable manner, shook our hands, or rather arms (a form of salutation peculiar to the American Indians) saying at the same time, "You are come." We followed him to an apartment prepared for the reception of guests. The pipe being filled, it is handed around: after which a large bowl, with what they call the "thin drink," is brought in and set down on a low table. In this bowl is a great wooden ladle; each person takes up in it as much as he pleases, and after drinking until satisfied, returns again into the bowl, pushing the handle toward the next person in the circle; and so it goes around.

Bartram, or Puc Puggy the "Flower Hunter" as he was known to the Indians, had on this day entered Cuscowilla with a party of white traders who had traveled overland from the St. Johns River to seal an agreement of trade with Cowkeeper and his people. Honey, beeswax, the hides of bears, deer, wolves, and tigers (in Bartram's words) would be bartered by the Indians for gingham and stroud cloth, glass beads, iron hatchets, knives, kettles, saddles, and horse tack, which by now had become necessities of Indian life.

But Cowkeeper, or Ahaya as he was known in the Hitchiti language, did not come to Florida as the result of Spanish enticement. An avowed enemy of Spain, the Cowkeeper had probably assisted James Oglethorpe in his attack on St. Augustine in 1740, perhaps then deciding to stay on in North Central Florida. Although the word *Seminole* was in common use by Bartram's time to refer generically to all former Creek Indians now residing in Florida, it is quite likely that the earliest use of the term was applied specifically to Cowkeeper's band, who had migrated south from the Oconee Creek vicinity of South Georgia to herd the free-ranging wild cattle descended from the Spanish herds of the old La Chua ranch. It was a case of "wild ones" herding wild ones, and the "cimarrones" to which the Spanish referred became "Seminoles" as pronounced in the Indian language.

In Creek country, two towns would often enter into an unusual kind of partnership for political and religious reasons. Each town was certain of having an ally or an opponent for ritualized political or ceremonial events. Such was the case with Cowkeeper's original Lachua settlement, named after the Spanish cattle ranch of La Chua and long defunct by Cowkeeper's arrival, but the source of the cattle herded by the Seminoles on the prairie.

1.4. Anthropologist John Goggin (*right*) and student standing in the Suwannee River at the Oven Hill site holding Seminole pottery vessel. Photo ca. 1958.

Some forty miles to the west, on the west side of the Suwannee River near present-day Old Town, was Cowkeeper's twin, so to speak, a village ruled by an Indian known as the White King. In 1764, a decade before Bartram, the trader Denys Rolle noted that the two towns were locked together in an Indian ball game lasting two weeks, during which time the participants consumed some eighteen casks of rum.

Like Cowkeeper's village, this Suwannee settlement has left little behind to be studied by the archaeologist. But from the depths of the river itself, near where the village must have been, came one of the most remarkable discoveries in all of Seminole archaeology. Here, in the early 1960s, the late University of Florida anthropologist John M. Goggin (fig. 1.4), working with the earliest scuba gear and a makeshift but serviceable barge, found the largest collection of Seminole pottery vessels known, sixteen of them complete or nearly complete, and dozens of other pottery sherds large enough for study.

Pottery from this site (fig. 1.5) is essentially Creek in form and style and cannot be readily distinguished from pottery from the Creek area of similar age. The brushed style of surface treatment, really a roughening of the soft clay surface with pine needles, dried grass, or corn cobs, connects the Seminoles to the Creek pottery tradition as surely as any historical document could. A detailed analysis of the size and shape of these vessels suggests a variety of uses by the Suwannee River Seminoles. Small round-bottomed bowls probably were used to serve individual portions of china-briar root soup, while larger carinated *casuela* bowls may have held meals of venison dressed with bear's oil. Large pottery bottles may have been used to store bear's oil and honey for seaborne trade with Spanish Cuba by means of large, ocean-going canoes. Not all of the Suwannee Seminole pottery showed strict conformance to Creek forms. Some of it appears to have been made to copy European forms, especially the Mediterranean olive jar, brought to the New World by the Spaniards and found at many mission sites.

European trade items found at the small land portion of the site identified by Goggin show that the early Seminoles participated in the colonial trade economy, however far removed they may have been from the real centers of trade at St. Augustine, St. Marks, Macon, and the trading houses of the St. Johns. Iron belt buckles, silver ear cones and earrings, glass beads, and horse tack indicate that individuals were able to trade for articles of personal adornment and thus represented a market for these items.

British military buttons, razors, knives, and gun parts likely represent diplomatic gifts to the Seminoles and suggest that the Suwannee town had some degree of political importance on the colonial frontier. Also found at the site was a spontoon tomahawk, similar to one proudly brandished by the Long Warrior, Cowkeeper's brother, in a portrait by William Bartram (fig. 1.6).

1.5. Pottery vessels from the Oven Hill site, Suwannee River, with style and form similar to Creek pottery. (In the collections of the Florida Museum of Natural History, Gainesville.)

1.6. William Bartram's drawing of the Long Warrior, published as an engraving for the frontispiece of the 1791 edition of Bartram's *Travels*. (Reproduced, with permission, from the 1955 Dover edition, edited by Mark van Doren.)

The Long Warrior sat as Cowkeeper's war chief or second in command, and he apparently lacked the composure of his brother. Once, when the Long Warrior and his band were refused credit at a St. Johns River trading post, he threatened the trader with a bolt of lightning sufficient to reduce his store to dust and ashes. When the trader called his bluff by challenging Long Warrior to call lightning down on a nearby live oak, both men turned diplomatic in an attempt to resolve their dispute. Both realized the far-reaching and entirely negative consequences of an interruption in trade.

Trade was so important to the early Seminoles that they moved their towns to seek more favorable locations for trading opportunities. By 1770 the original Suwannee town was abandoned by White King and relocated to the east bank of the river at a place called Talahasochte. This meant that trade caravans could come and go from the village without having to ford the Suwannee River, which could be unpredictably treacherous. At about the same time Cowkeeper abandoned his original town on the Alachua savanna and founded Cuscowilla. Bartram reports that the stench of rotten fish drove them away, sufficient cause indeed for relocation. But if a new trade route had been established from the St. Johns River to Talahasochte, certainly Cowkeeper would not want to have been bypassed.

Whatever other reasons may have led to the move to Cuscowilla, the fact that a murder occurred in the Alachua village in 1764 may have set the stage for the abandonment of the original Seminole village. In that year, Cowkeeper's young nephew (son of the ill-tempered Long Warrior?), in a drunken rage, grabbed a glass liquor bottle and bashed out the brains of another Indian. The horrified inhabitants would not bury the corpse and moved their houses away from the spot where it lay.

The town plans of Cuscowilla and Talahasochte were organized around a central square or squareground, as was traditional in Creek society. Bartram gives us a good description of the Seminole squaregrounds, based on his visits to both Cuscowilla and Talahasochte. Such towns consisted of at least three cabins or pavilions arranged around a public square. The royal cabin, where the "king" or chief, his war leader, and other advisors sat, faced east. Other important men from the town sat in a cabin facing north, while visitors and others were placed in a cabin facing south. Individual households in these main towns were also built around the squareground plan, with two or more buildings in use by a single family opening on to a small central courtyard.

Life and Death among the Alachua Seminoles

For most Seminoles, however, daily life took place well away from the hustle and bustle of the central squareground town. Although the towns of Cuscowilla and Talahasochte remain archaeologically invisible, archaeological evidence of a small Seminole farmstead has come to light. Above the west shore of Newnans Lake (once known as Lake Pithlachucco, or "canoe place"), in what archaeologist William Sears called the smallest archaeological site he ever had the pleasure to excavate, were found the remains of a circular structure about eighteen feet in diameter. Associated with the building (evidence of which consisted of a dark circular stain and six postholes) were pottery sherds from seven to nine vessels, one projectile point, and two fragments of a trade pipe. The particular style of rim decoration found on the pottery sherds, rare in other Florida Seminole collections, is identical to the style seen on sherds found at the Spalding trading post on the lower St. Johns River.

Not found at the Pithlachucco site in any abundance are the popular trade goods so sought after by the Seminoles, leaving us to ponder the possibility that the city folks at Cuscowilla ended up with all the goods. (I am told that Sears entertained the idea that this was the location of Cuscowilla, being none too trusting of the map of the site drawn by Bartram—if so, that means that the large field in which the site was found should contain many more like it.)

One place trade goods ended up was buried with the deceased, either as grave offerings or personal possessions meant to go on to the next world. Road construction in the 1950s along the east side of Paynes Prairie unearthed two such burials. Excavation by John Goggin and his students determined that one Seminole man had been laid flexed on his left side, head facing east, with an iron trade tomahawk and an iron knife on his chest and a glass mirror tucked under his knees. Three powder and shot pouches had been placed by his legs. Around his waist was a leather buckled belt; just above his heels was an inverted brass kettle.

Tucked behind the man's back were two more brass buckles, several coils of copper wire, red and yellow paint, an iron file and rasp and an iron knife, two pocket knives, and a gun lock (fig. 1.7). To obtain these items, this man would have had to turn in a minimum of thirty-four pounds of deerskins. In a good year, this amount could readily have come from less than one season in the woods, as hunters were known to average about forty pounds of skins per year. For one pound of skins, forty bullets or five strings of beads could be had; for five pounds, a gingham shirt; for eighteen pounds, a gun; and for sixty pounds, a saddle. This man and 8,000 or so other hunters in the lower Southeast brought in more than 300,000 skins a year during the height of the deerskin trade.

As individual Seminole hunters learned the ropes of the deerskin trade, the traditional role of the chief diminished in importance. With the decline in chiefly authority and power came a decline in the use of the squareground. With the death of Cowkeeper in 1784, the control of the Alachua band passed to his nephew (or son), the man for whom Paynes Prairie is named. King Payne, as he was called, resided not at Cuscowilla (which was, apparently, abandoned) but instead at the new settlement called Paynestown, in the southeast corner of what is now Paynes Prairie State Preserve. Cuscowilla was a squareground town, Paynestown was not. Archaeological investigations at Paynestown indicate that it was organized more like a typical Southern plantation than like a traditional Creek or Seminole squareground town.

Around the area of the main house were found concentrations of English ceramics dating to the period 1790–1820, sherds of glass, glass necklace beads, gun parts, and brushed Seminole pottery. Surrounding the house in discrete clusters were additional concentrations of English ceramics, Semi-

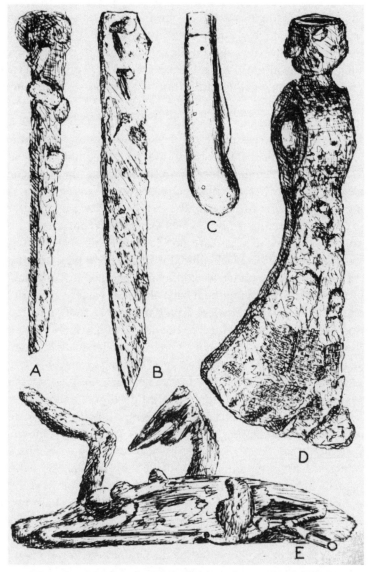

1.7. Selected artifacts from the Zetrouer site Seminole burial, Paynes Prairie vicinity, as illustrated by Goggin et al. in *Florida Anthropologist* 2 (1949). Artifacts are currently curated at the Florida Museum of Natural History, Gainesville. (Reproduced with the permission of the Florida Anthropological Society.)

nole pottery, more glass beads, and a silver earring, possibly marking the locations of outbuildings associated with the main house or associated refuse pits. Payne was clearly a man of some wealth, built not only on the deerskin trade but probably also on the sale or trade of cattle allowed to range on the prairie. In 1793 Payne was reported to have possessed twenty slaves, fifteen hundred head of cattle, four hundred horses, and innumerable sheep and goats.

Ultimately the success and prosperity of the Alachua Seminoles led to their demise. Their successful efforts at husbandry demonstrated to the land-hungry Americans that interior Florida did indeed hold the potential to turn a profit. The Seminole wealth on the hoof and their agricultural surpluses stored away in corn cribs and potato houses made tempting targets for groups of border ruffians. In 1812 Paynestown was under attack by a group of Georgia militia led by Colonel Daniel Newnan, part of a larger U.S.-inspired offensive to seize East Florida from Spain. The eighty-year-old Payne, assisted by his black allies, his brother Bowlegs, and the two hundred some warriors under his command launched a flank attack on the militia, eventually driving them back along the eastern shore of Lake Pithlachucco in defeat. Nonetheless, Payne sustained a mortal wound and soon died. Mourning his dead brother, Bowlegs is said to have proclaimed: "I shall wrap you in a robe and hoist you to a slender scaffold where the whistling winds shall take you to the happy hunting ground."

Thus began the diaspora of the Alachua Seminoles. Bowlegs moved to the Suwannee River, where he had the misfortune of encountering General Andrew Jackson's invading force in 1818. This time Bowlegs moved deeper into the Florida interior, settling for a time east of Tampa before moving on. By 1821 he was dead. Seminole Blacks associated with the Alachua Seminoles went south to the remote swamps of the Withlacoochee or to the new settlement of Peliklakaha, in the rolling savanna land of West Central Florida. Leadership of the band passed from Payne to his eldest nephew and then quickly, upon his premature death, to Micanopy, the younger nephew of Payne. Micanopy moved to Okahumpka, in Central Florida's Lake County, from where he would be drawn into the Second Seminole War and eventually, in 1838, deported to Indian Territory.

Small groups of Seminoles lingered in the old Alachua area or perhaps sought it out as a temporary refuge on their move south. At the Seminole town of San Falasco located somewhere in the great hammock of that name northwest of present Gainesville, white observers in the early 1820s would witness Seminole men and women dancing at night on the hard, beaten earth of the dance ground. The men, faces painted to resemble whiskers, and the women, wearing leg rattles made of terrapin shells filled with pebbles, danced and whooped around the dance fire, singing a "wild" song. It is interesting that the chief of San Falasco village was also a blacksmith and hammered out silver coins into ornaments.

But never again would the Seminole heartland see the thriving native society so vividly described by Bartram, nor would it see bands of the "wild ones" stalking the hammocks for deer or driving cattle through the grass of the Paynes Prairie. Although dispersed settlement occurred in the area through the early years of the Second Seminole War and the southern bands considered it part of their territory, effective control over the area was lost with the departure of Micanopy. Cowkeeper came to the great savanna as a Creek, his descendant Micanopy left as a Seminole.

Seminoles in the Tallahassee Red Hills

The story of the northern Seminole bands is also one of separation, nucleation, and dispersal. The geographical setting was the Tallahassee Red Hills, abrupt clay uplands dissected by stream valleys and prairie wetlands, east of the present location of Tallahassee. This was the former center of the Apalachee mission province, Spain's failed breadbasket for the mission colony. The Apalachee Indians encountered here by the conquistador Hernando de Soto in 1539 were not too different in culture from the Creeks he would encounter later in his trek; indeed they belonged more to that culture area than to the Timucua to their east. For the Lower Creeks who came to settle here at Spanish invitation in the mid-1700s, the move was short and the territory familiar. Brim's son Secoffee was one of the first immigrants and, like Cowkeeper to the south, he became a central figure in the transformation of Creek to Seminole. Unlike Cowkeeper, who bragged of killing at least eighty-six Spaniards in his day, Secoffee considered himself to be a friend of Spain and encouraged other bands to occupy the area between Tallahassee and the post at St. Marks. Also unlike Cowkeeper, Secoffee had no Bartram to record his deeds and demeanor for posterity; thus he is poorly known to history and anthropology. By the time that Secoffee passed away in 1785, one year after Cowkeeper, both the British and the Spanish recognized that the bands in the old Apalachee area were acting independently of the Creek Confederacy, or as a separate part of it. In 1823, when pressures exerted by the U.S. policy of Indian removal forced unified action between the eastern and western divisions of Seminoles, it was Neamathla, chief of a town on the Apalachicola River, who was chosen to represent Seminole interests at the Treaty of Moultrie Creek. For his co-operation, Neamathla was given a small reserve in his home area while the rest of the Seminoles agreed, or so thought the Americans, to move within the boundaries of a new reservation created in the central portion of the peninsula. These Apalachicola Seminoles were dealt with separately by the federal government, but by 1838 they had given up their claim and threw their lot in with the rest of the Florida Seminoles.

How Did the Seminoles Become Seminole?

How did the Seminoles become Seminole? There are many answers, but no single one. As a political body, the Seminoles began to achieve indepen-dence from the Creeks with the actions of Cowkeeper as early as 1765. The term *Seminole* comes into common use at about that time. Certainly by 1818 the breach between Creek and Seminole was permanent and absolute as the Lower Creeks assisted the Americans in strikes against the Seminoles in the First Seminole War. But saying that the Florida Indians were function-ing apart from the Creeks is not the same thing as saying they were acting as a unified polity unto themselves. So a second question becomes, When did the Seminoles begin acting as Seminoles? Factionalism dominated the history of the various Seminole bands in Florida, some pro-British, some pro-Spanish, others staunchly opportunistic. The strongest evidence for political unity comes during the early American period, and this only un-der duress. When forced to make treaties with the United States, the Semi-noles could give the appearance of political unity, just as the Creeks had done with the Creek Confederacy. But the results were never satisfactory. Appointed spokesmen or head chiefs were figureheads with no real lasting authority and compelled no compliance with treaty demands. Agreements made under such circumstances were bound to fail, and fail they did, as we will see in chapter 3.

Political unity is only one measure of the development of Seminole iden-tity. The Seminoles and Miccosukees of today are known for their strong sense of cultural self-identity. They know what it means to be Seminole and think of themselves in this way. Politics aside, when did a Seminole cultural identity emerge? When did Florida Seminole culture become unique, dis-tinct from its Creek ancestry? What features made it so? When did the Seminoles themselves recognize it as such? As with many questions an-thropologists ask, the answers are elusive and likely to be controversial when they do come. Not everyone will agree, particularly when key evidence is based on observations by outsiders—military men, government officials, intellectuals—rather than by the voices of the Seminoles. If only such testimony existed! Sadly, the realities of modern life have conspired to break the chain of Seminole oral history. Threads remain, but the fabric is not whole. Like the patchwork for which the Seminoles are famous, oral testimony must be pieced together with swatches pulled from the historical, archaeological, and anthropological records. When this is done, a pattern emerges, once again showing the Seminoles responding to stress.

The source of the stress was the Second Seminole War, fought between 1835 and 1842. The objective of the war for the Americans was the forcible removal of the Seminoles from Florida. The hostilities would sever many Seminoles from their villages and fields and disrupt their fundamental way of life. For the Seminoles, the choices were clear: Surrender, fight, or flee. Those who survived and remained in Florida did so, I will argue, because they found strength in a new and revitalized cultural identity, an identity as Seminole. This identity owed much to the infusion of Red Stick Creeks into Florida following the Creek War of 1814, who brought with them the words of Tecumseh and the nativistic influences of the Indian prophets. The themes of resistance and revival as they relate to the emergence of a Seminole cultural identity will be further explored in chapter 3. A related key element arising from the Second Seminole War is the increasing importance of the medicine bundle in the annual busk ritual, discussed in chapter 5.

The Seminoles Make Themselves

It has often been written in the scholarly literature on the Seminoles and other southeastern Indians of the historic period that their desire for European or American trade goods became a dependency such that they willingly gave up the ways of their own culture and accepted the values of the white man. Indeed, the archaeology of this period is much concerned with mapping the spread of these so-called trade goods as they infiltrate native material culture and with determining the specific contexts in which these objects are found at individual archaeological sites. The overall trend in the years following initial European contact seems to be that glass beads, axes, mirrors, scissors, and other exotic objects probably obtained by the Indians as gifts are first found in burial mounds, then, through time, become part of the domestic refuse deposits in village sites. Creek Indian archaeological sites of the eighteenth century typically contain abundant European objects in both village and burial contexts, obtained in exchange for deerskins, pelts, and perhaps livestock and produce. Looking strictly at the level of the artifact, it would be logical to conclude that the replacement of aboriginal material culture by introduced objects of European origin was widespread and rapid and that it nearly wiped out any traces of indigenous technology.

But here we must question the simple logic that equates changes in artifacts to changes in culture. Most archaeologists have long abandoned simplistic models of acculturation, the process of culture change in which one culture adopts the lifeways of another, but the tendency to think this way still is strong and appears in museum exhibits, in the popular media, and even in college classrooms. Using an iron axe instead of one made of stone may indicate fundamental changes in traditional patterns of procuring raw materials and age-old networks of trade but does not necessarily indicate that the Indians desired to be more like the whites or had abandoned their own values and beliefs—likewise wearing glass beads instead of those made of shell, or using a flintlock instead of the bow and arrow. To be sure, each trade item in its own way expresses some change in aboriginal culture. But do the items, either together or singly, reflect fundamental changes in the values and attitudes of traditional Indian culture? That the southeastern Indians would be drawn into an intricate web of interactions with the various European colonists (and ultimately the Americans) was unavoidable. That changing artifact inventories from purely aboriginal to almost completely introduced items reflects aspects of the complex interactions between white man and Indian is a secure and unassailable premise of historical archaeological research. Certainly many of the interactions were driven by Indian motivations, Indian strategies for acting in their own best interest in their dealings with the unpredictable and power-hungry colonists. History tells us that the colonists were often shrewd and canny in their dealings with the natives. That same history tells us, between the lines, that the Indians met them move for move. Both sides manipulated circumstances to their best advantage, both were savvy at playing political games.

It was not because of inconvenience that Cowkeeper was absent from the Congress at Picolata, where the British colonial authorities met with the Creek chiefs to work out terms of land cession. He had only to travel a short distance east from his home above the Alachua savanna to the banks of the St. Johns River. Yet he would wait several months and travel to St. Augustine with his own retinue to strike his own deal with the colonials.

Clearly the Seminoles and the other historic southeastern Indian peoples were not subdued or pacified by trinkets or baubles of European trade. Culture change did indeed occur; this cannot be denied. But the Seminoles, Creeks, Choctaws, Tunicas, Natchez, and others did at times use trade goods to maintain and reinforce traditional means of prestige reckoning, status distinctions, and ritual concern for the dead. The horse and the firearm enabled the Indian warrior to achieve his status, albeit under different circumstances than his prehistoric ancestors. The brightly colored clothes, silver earrings, crescent gorgets, and multicolored strings of beads were as likely physical expressions of success as they were indications of wanting to be like the white man. On occasion, the symbolic meaning of clothing or personal ornamentation was used with a great sense of irony by the Indians. Seminoles seen on the front lines of Second Seminole War battles wearing standard military issue blue jackets taken from army dead were probably not mimicking the authority of military officers in the eyes of their fellow warriors but rather taunting the soldiers with their likely fate.

Rather than being merely the passive recipients of the white man's culture, cast in the role of helpless victims in the path of insurmountable historical change, the Seminoles are perhaps better understood as a culture always fully capable of creating their own identity, ready to reinvent themselves in the face of new challenges by combining innovation and tradition.

→ 2 ←

Camp and Clan

↑ ↑ ↑ ↑ ↑ ↑ ↑ ↑ ↑ ↑ ↑ ↑ ↑

The world of the Seminole Indian was the world of the mothers and grand-mothers. From birth in the mother's clan camp to childhood and adolescence under the watchful eyes of aunts and uncles, through adulthood and its responsibilities back to the camp, the life of the Seminole was deeply connected to an extended family related through the mother's lineage. Every Seminole was born into the mother's clan, a system known as matrilineal to anthropologists. This means that rights, responsibilities, and obligations were passed down through the mother's line. Clan membership was the single most important way in which an individual related to the rest of society. Persons always knew where they stood; they were members of the Bear, Panther, Wind, or Snake clan, and as such they understood how they must behave with regard to other clan members and what their roles as clan members were in a society composed of many clans.

Most important for an archaeological consideration of Seminole clans is the fact that family-sized segments of a clan were organized into discrete geographical units of residence. These are the "clan camps" of recent anthropological literature, the *istihapo*, about which Alexander Spoehr wrote among the Cow Creek Seminoles (today's Brighton Reservation) (fig. 2.1), and the *huti* of the ancestral Creeks. Matrilocal residence meant that after marriage, the new couple would take up residence near the camp of the wife's mother and would "live and eat in common," in the words of one chronicler, with the mother, the mother's sisters, and the wife's own married sisters, who, like herself, brought their husbands back to the clan camp.

How far back into southeastern prehistory clan camps go is, of course, not certain, but it is tempting to think of the farmsteads of the Mississippian chiefdoms identified by archaeologists in their surveys of uplands along river drainages as ancestral. Certainly by the mid-1700s the settlement pattern of dispersed related family homesteads organized around central

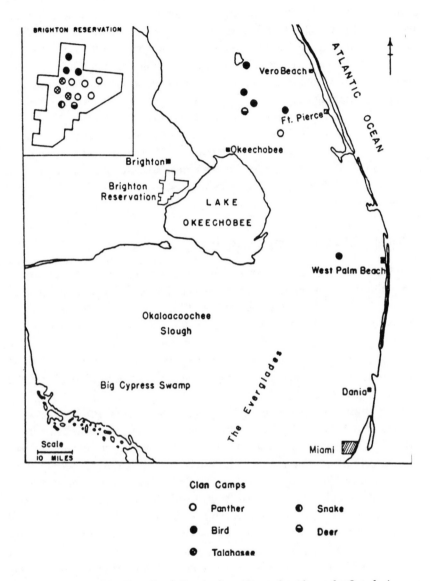

2.1. Clan camps of the Cow Creek Seminole as drawn by Alexander Spoehr in 1941. (Originally published in the Field Museum of Natural History's *Anthropological Series* no. 33, 11.)

squareground towns, or *talwa*, was typical for the Creek area of middle Alabama. The communities formed by the households of related women were called huti in the Creek area, according to informants of the anthropologist John R. Swanton. Huti referred not only to the physical setting of the household but also to the economic responsibilities and obligations that bound the households together. Tasks such as planting and harvesting garden crops, making pots, baskets, mats, and clothing were shared by members of the huti, as were the responsibilities of raising children.

As the huti of the Creeks were drawn together around the talwa, or squareground towns, so were the istihapo or clan camps of the later Seminoles drawn together around the busk grounds. But the historical path from huti to istihapo was not necessarily straight; indeed, much of it is hidden from view.

What Would a Clan Camp Look Like?

Can we develop a social history of the Seminole clan camp? What important cultural or historical events influenced the form and function of clans among the Seminoles? Unfortunately, until the mid-twentieth century, anthropological observations of the Seminoles were few and are insufficient to answer these questions. We can, however, look to the combined evidence of archaeology and ethnohistory to bring forth part of the story. We must begin by asking the question, Can Seminole clan camps be identified in the archaeological record?

On a sandy ridge overlooking Newnans Lake east of Gainesville, not far from the north rim of Paynes Prairie, were the remains of a small Seminole camp that contained at least one post-supported structure and a dark-stained activity area some six meters in diameter (site A296, see fig. 1.3). Archaeologists John Goggin and William Sears were led to the spot by a local high school youth who had found some pottery sherds protruding from the surface. Their subsequent excavations in the area of the surface-collected pottery revealed a concentration of Seminole artifacts located within a dark midden stain just barely below the ground surface.

Most of the 679 pottery sherds recovered were of the type Chattahoochee Brushed, the typical brushed-surface pottery associated with eighteenth- and nineteenth-century Creek and Seminole occupation. Other artifacts included two pieces of a trade pipe stem and one projectile point. But it was the pottery sherds that most interested Sears, particularly the ways in which the rims of the pots had been decorated. Besides the plain rim sherds, Sears noticed that all other rims were notched or angled at the

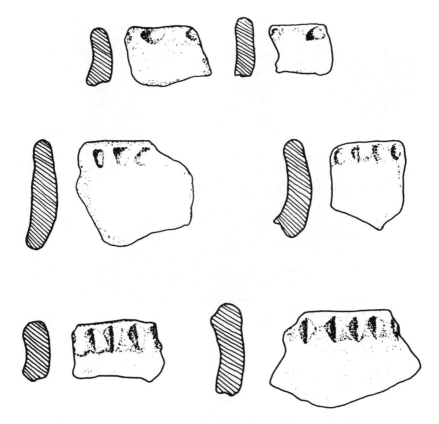

2.2. Pottery rim styles from various Seminole sites in North Florida.

top of the rim. Further, rim notching was not confined to a single vessel form but was found on sherds belonging most likely to both jars and bowls. Therefore, the presence of rim notching was not strictly a functional matter but may have been a matter of style or preference (fig. 2.2). If so, Sears wondered, what would have been the social context of this preference? To what element of cultural reality did variations in rim treatment correlate?

Given that the women of a clan camp shared not only tasks and responsibilities but also a common identity as clan members, it is plausible that this common identity was physically expressed using specific and distinct styles of pottery rim decoration. This means that each clan camp would have made its own style of pottery rim, perhaps similar to that of other camps of the same clan but distinct from all other camps. Archaeologically, this is a testable proposition. Single clan camps should have only a single rim style (or a tight set of related styles). Conversely, archaeological sites

2.3. Pottery rim styles from the middle Suwannee River in the vicinity of Talahasochte and Oven Hill in the archaeological collections of the Florida Museum of
Natural History, Gainesville.

that are presumed to represent towns should have, in the aggregate, many
different styles of pottery rim treatment (although, if properly and ideally
excavated, would again reveal distinct styles associated with each household square within the town).

Unfortunately, the town of Cuscowilla, with which Sears's homestead
site is almost certainly associated, has not been archaeologically identified.
But from the depths of the Suwannee River, at a place called Oven Hill east
of the present location of Old Town, comes a remarkable collection of Seminole Indian pottery (fig. 2.3) belonging, most likely, to a Seminole town
located on the west bank of the river in the 1760s. Here, working with scuba
gear from a customized diving barge, John Goggin and his University of
Florida students collected the largest assemblage of Seminole pottery vessels known, including at least four distinct rim styles. This is what we
would expect from a squareground town such as Bartram and other observers say existed during this time.

Moving ahead to the period of the Second Seminole War we find that
most Seminole towns are no longer organized around a squareground

(Osceola's wartime village at Powell's Town being an exception) but instead appear to be loose aggregates of households spread out over many acres. Such a village existed on the sandy uplands on the south shore of the Lake Tsala Apopka chain, east of the present town of Floral City. Military documents show this to have been an extensive village, its two halves separated by a black creek but joined by an "Indian footbridge." Where once the board houses of this village stood, now orange trees grow and backyard gardens thrive (fig. 2.4). Archaeological surveys and limited excavations in the mid-1980s showed that, indeed, each household was marked by its own thin deposit of archaeological trash. One excavation revealed what was likely a cooking area associated with one of the households. Most of what the archaeologists found were broken pieces of pottery, but there were also bottle glass, iron tools and utensils, and several military buttons. Pottery rim sherds were collected from three of the household deposits, each showing a distinctive style of rim notching.

Perhaps Seminole clan camps can be discovered through archaeology. If so, this should not be so surprising. It is not difficult to imagine that people who share a strong common identity would want to express that identity

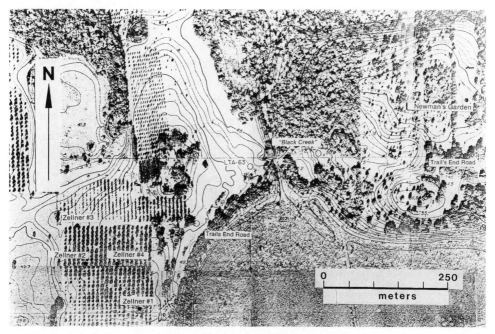

2.4. Aerial view of the archaeological sites on the Newman and Zellner properties, presumed clan camps of a dispersed Seminole village during the Second Seminole War.

2.5. Diamond pattern sewn in seed beads on a garter excavated with a Seminole burial from the Fort Brooke cemetery, Tampa. (Photograph courtesy of Harry M. and Jacquelyn G. Piper.)

through some material means. Pottery styles would be the longest lasting and the most easily discovered and recognized by archaeologists. But other aspects of material culture may have been used to signal clan affiliation as well, although perhaps not surviving as readily in the archaeological record. Designs in beadwork, such as the diamondback rattlesnake motif embroidered on the man's garter excavated at the Fort Brooke cemetery, may have been used in this way (fig. 2.5).

Continuity and Change in Seminole Clans

Even if the archaeological evidence suggests that clan camps can be identified in an archaeological record that spans the period of the initial Seminole settlement of Florida through the Second Seminole War, what can we know about the changes in the structure and function of the clans themselves during this time? Economic conditions in the period from British to Spanish to American rule of Florida pressured Seminole society to decentralize, for several reasons. With more traders moving inland through the territory and more trading houses opening up along the St. Johns River and on well-traveled interior trails near Seminole towns, the squareground town and its chief became less integral to successful trade relations. A trader could simply strike up a deal with individual families encountered in the outlying camps and even entice them to travel to established stores to trade on their own. Such may have been the case with the household that once occupied the site above Newnans Lake, described previously. Rim sherds with an identical notched style to those found by William Sears were found by John Goggin in later work at Spalding's Lower Store on the St. Johns. These two occurrences of this rim style are the only known at present in Seminole archaeology, suggesting some connection between the Newnan site and the Spalding trading house.

Another force was at work both to place power, authority, and prestige in the hands of the individual Seminole and to strike at the very institution of matrilineal inheritance. This was the accumulation of personal wealth among those Seminoles who were successful at playing the trading game. In Seminole society, a man's rights and obligations were passed down to him through his mother's line. Because a man was a member of his mother's clan, this meant that his own sons could not inherit from him. Instead, a man had this special relationship with his nephews, the sons of his siblings, who were members of the same clan. The transfer of political power followed these lines, or so the evidence suggests. Cowkeeper's nephew, Payne, became the next chief of the Alachua band after Cowkeeper's death. Micanopy, nephew of Payne, eventually became the chief of the band and, some say, lead ruler of the Seminoles at the outset of the Second Seminole War. Likewise a married man, whose residence would be in the vicinity of his wife's family, would from time to time return to his own mother's camp to help with agricultural tasks and other family responsibilities.

This system functioned smoothly in the years before the trading economy flourished. But once the colonists desired not only the deerskins hauled in by the Indians but the meat from their herds and produce from their fields, the opportunity existed for individual Seminoles to become wealthy by the standards of the time. With wealth came a strong desire to keep it and its source within the control of the nuclear family, from father to son. Thus we see that by 1823 Opauney, a Seminole living in the lake district of Central Florida near present-day Winter Haven, whose fortune rested on a thriving rice export business to St. Augustine, upon his death left his wealth both in cash ($7,000) and possessions to his son. Even so, Opauney, like many Seminoles, lived with a foot in both worlds, traditional and modern. Although his plantation resembled in most respects a typical southern plantation of the day with its two-story frame house, corn house, dairy, and stable, it also contained a "physic" house, where sacred war medicines were kept for use by the medicine man. Although Opauney's son inherited his property and movable wealth, his houses, orchards of peaches, and fields of corn and rice were destroyed in keeping with Indian custom.

In the years prior to the Second Seminole War, during British rule and the subsequent era of the second Spanish period, the economic stimulus of the market had a powerful effect on the transformation of Seminole society. Through time, the power of the squareground chiefs eroded. There would be no more Cowkeepers after his death in the 1780s. Towns became less populated, Seminole households more far flung. Maintaining clan relationships became a difficult proposition. Yet the Seminole clans did not disappear. Ethnographers of the twentieth century write of the central importance of clans to Florida Seminole life, to Seminole ritual and ceremony. Were there events or circumstances that acted to strengthen the position of the clans in Seminole culture?

Although it may at first seem counter to common sense, the possibility exists that the stress and disruption brought on by the Second Seminole War revitalized social ties and cultural traditions among the Seminoles rather than causing their demise. To survive, Seminoles needed to connect with other Seminoles, rekindling bonds, forming groups from which sufficient numbers of warriors could be drawn, groups to plan and coordinate strategies of economic self-sufficiency and spiritual well-being. In this context a reactivation of clan bonds makes sense, as a traditional way of keeping dispersed groups connected. Of course, documentary support for this process is either nonexistent or cannot be directly interpreted. Archaeological support fares little better.

Not conclusive by any means, evidence contained in the archaeological record does at least provoke some new ways of thinking about the role of clans among the Seminoles of the Second Seminole War. Beneath a city parking garage in present-day downtown Tampa rested the remains of Seminole Indians who died awaiting deportation to Indian Territory (fig. 2.6). During archaeological excavations at the site by Piper Archaeological Research prior to the construction of the garage, the graves of thirteen adult Seminole men, eight Seminole women, and nineteen adolescents, teenagers, or children were identified. These graves were not randomly located in the larger cemetery area but appear to have been intentionally interred in at least five burial groups or plots, based on consistent regular alignment of the grave pits in each group (fig. 2.7). At least one child in each group was buried with an extraordinary amount of grave goods, items unlikely for them to have possessed (at least in these quantities) in life.

2.6. The Fort Brooke parking garage, built over the former burial site of Seminole Indians who died while encamped at Fort Brooke awaiting deportation to Indian Territory during the Second Seminole War.

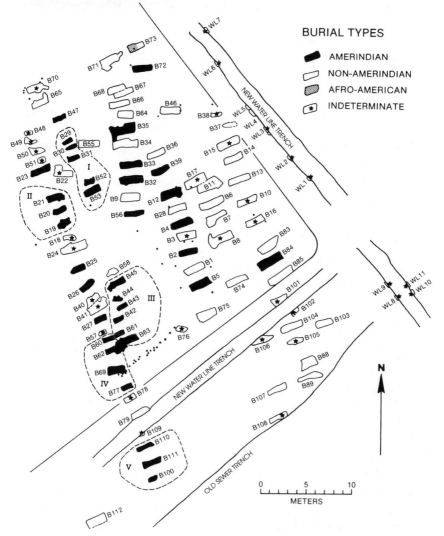

BURIAL TYPES

AMERINDIAN
NON-AMERINDIAN
AFRO-AMERICAN
INDETERMINATE

2.7. Archaeological plan of excavated Seminole burials in the Fort Brooke cemetery, grouped according to possible clan association. (Based on a map drawn by Harry M. and Jacquelyn G. Piper in 1982, with burial groups added by the author.)

In Burial Group # 1 (Burial # 30), a four- to six-year-old youth was buried with two iron cups, an iron knife in a copper case, six perforated coins (dated 1821–1839, including Spanish reales and U.S. dimes), a metal bodice piece, a fragment of an earring, two brass button fragments, and more than three hundred glass beads. In Burial Group # 3 (Burial # 61), an infant no more than eighteen months old was buried with two white metal earrings, two perforated coins, two white metal bodice pieces, and literally thousands of seed and necklace beads. Similar assemblages were found with children in all groups (fig. 2.8).

When compared with the items found with an adult male in Burial Group # 5 (Burial # 111), consisting of one iron arrowhead, one bodice piece, a gun flint and ramrod fragment, a copper wire coil, five flat copper sheets, and one whetstone, the pattern of behavior becomes quite clear. To account for the large numbers of grave goods buried with the young, archaeologists Harry and Jacquelyn Piper suggested the intriguing, and plausible, explanation that the clans were seeking to establish alliances among themselves by distributing gifts to their deceased youths. This effort would have been equally adaptive for those groups remaining in Florida and those facing deportation into unknown circumstances. Whatever the case, clan structure remained strong in Florida and was one aspect of Seminole culture consistently noted by outside observers. Wrote government anthropologist Gene Sterling in 1936: "The importance of the clan in Seminole life cannot be overemphasized. It is still the dominant social unit that exerts a profound influence on all phases of native life. It dictates the economic as well as the social."

Eight clans exist in the modern Seminole Tribe: Bear, Panther, Wind, Otter, Snake, Bird, Deer, and Big Town (sometimes called Toad or Frog). In 1939, the anthropologist Alexander Spoehr recorded the Panther, Bird, Talahasee, Snake, and Deer clans among the Cow Creek band, ancestors of today's Brighton Reservation population of Muskogee speakers. Members of the Otter, Bear, and Talwalako (Big Town) clans lived with the Cow Creek band, although their origins were with the Mikasuki bands. Thus there is a high degree of consistency with the present day, although we cannot expect this always to have been the case. In the 1890s Charles Cory observed that many Seminole clans said once to have existed had become extinct, such as the Eagle clan of the legendary Osceola. His list of clans then still active shows that extinctions continued to occur, perhaps rapidly, through the 1930s. Cory's list includes Rattlesnake, Alligator, Panther, Big Blue Heron, Little Black Snake, Bear, Wind, Otter, Little Yellow Bird, Wolf, Frog, Little Blackbird, Wildcat, and Deer, among others. He noted that the

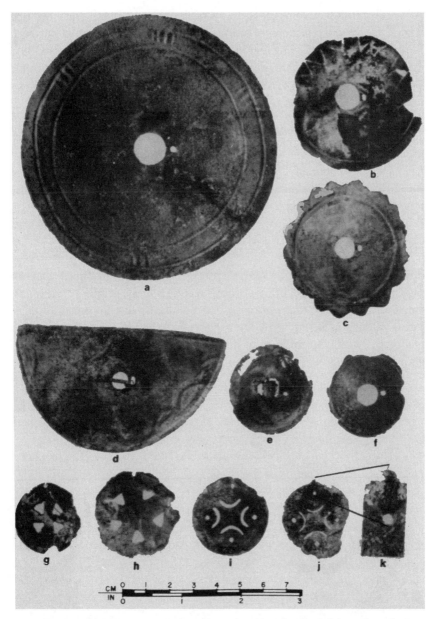

2.8. White metal bodice pieces and pendants found with subadult burials at the Fort Brooke cemetery. (Reproduced with the permission of Harry M. and Jacquelyn G. Piper.)

Alligator, Little Black Snake, and Crocodile clans were gone or would be soon. Clearly, the pantheon of animals used and the association between clan names and myths or tribal histories were once much richer than they are now. It is also clear that individual clans have specific historical origins and reflect a dynamic process of formulation, growth, and extinction or regrouping.

Clan structure among the Seminoles allowed for some flexibility in social relationships as the population grew or declined or moved from place to place. Yet it also provided the fundamental structure and continuity as a basis for social change. Overall, the effect of the clan system was one of stability. As individuals, the Seminoles could expect that their place in the world would be defined in more or less regular ways by the clan system. When Seminoles entered the wage labor force in the 1940s picking and canning vegetables, they did so along clan lines.

One of the strongest lines of continuity appears to have been passing down the role of medicine man through the Panther (or Tiger) clan, an association preserved in oral traditions recounting the origins of the medicine bundles among the Seminoles. The Seminoles lived in a world given form, value, and meaning by the existence of the clans. Today, there is a resurgence in the importance of the clan, as individual clans hold annual gatherings to renew friendships and rekindle the old clan stories.

→ **3** ←

Red Sticks, White Plumes

↑ ↑ ↑ ↑ ↑ ↑ ↑ ↑ ↑ ↑ ↑ ↑ ↑

Cultures on a Collision Course

The years between 1812 and 1858 were filled with nearly incessant hostilities and tensions between the Seminoles and the citizens, soldiers, and government of the United States. Historians know well the causes of these conflicts. Manifest Destiny had much to do with it. Florida, Land of Flowers, was an attractive prize for a new country already restless. Certainly, Florida was no place for Spain to be, and it was not right that the Indians should have it. Although outright anti-Indian sentiments were not commonly expressed, many, including Andrew Jackson, felt that Indian Removal was the humane thing to do. A final collision of cultures was inevitable they said, and the Red Man was destined to lose. The peculiar institution of slavery as it applied to Africans had already been accommodated into the American worldview, but that worldview had difficulty contemplating yet another underclass, made up of American Indians. And there could be no separate but equal. If destiny guided human affairs, and it most surely did, then this much was certain: the Seminoles had to go.

The political consequences of this philosophy were very real. When Florida became a territory of the United States in 1821, about five thousand Seminoles had homes there, in villages dispersed from the Apalachicola drainage through the Tallahassee Red Hills to the Central Florida prairies. By 1858, less than forty years later, fewer than two hundred Seminoles remained, and these were now hidden away in small camps in the most remote areas of the South Florida wetlands.

But the removal of the Seminoles from Florida involved more than just territorial expansion. Like the quest for land, this cause also resulted from a concern for property. This property was in the form of human beings, African slaves brought by planters to low country Carolina and Georgia to work the rice fields or cotton plantations. Having Spanish Florida as a convenient escape hatch was one problem. But it was even more aggravating when the escaped slaves disappeared in the Florida swamps beyond the grasp of the slave catcher, harbored by Indians who could be considered armed and dangerous.

Had the Seminoles been acting out of a desire to provide personal freedom for the slaves, things may have worked out differently. Instead, the Seminoles looked upon the Africans as their property, which meant they yielded them only through force. Slavery was a concept familiar to the southeastern Indians, but it resulted from the spoils of war, not from attitudes of racial superiority. But in the aboriginal Southeast, slaves such as the escaped Africans did have value and could be exchanged under the right circumstances once agreeable terms had been settled on. If the economic realities of the early nineteenth century meant that the value of slaves was determined in dollars, so be it. If pressed, then, it was dollars the Seminoles wanted for their African vassals. This enraged the slave owners and added to their fears that an Indian-African alliance would threaten their power. As long as there were Seminoles in Spanish Florida, the institution of plantation slavery in the lower Southeast would not be safe.

After the United States gained Florida in 1821, this aspect of the slavery issue became less of a problem. At the least an international boundary would not have to be crossed to retrieve lost property. Still the government blundered badly by failing to recognize the strength of the bond between African and Seminole. This, as we shall see, was the single most important immediate cause of the Second Seminole War.

The historical outline of the war years is well known. Spain's failure to rule its colony with authority coupled with American territorial aggressiveness meant that border conflict was inevitable. In 1816 the Americans established Fort Scott on the Flint River, perched only a few miles above Spanish Florida and on the bank opposite Neamathla's village at Fowltown. The logical supply route to the fort, said the United States, was via the Apalachicola River northward through Spanish territory. One slight obstacle to this passage was the so-called Negro Fort, on the Apalachicola about halfway between the gulf and Fort Scott. This location was occupied by 334 blacks, well armed, and decidedly anti-American. When the attempted passage of supplies to Fort Scott was indeed challenged by the black force on July 27, 1816, they were quickly dispatched by a lucky hotshot to the powder magazine from an American gunboat.

The next year saw an attack launched on Fowltown from Fort Scott by the noted Indian fighter Edmund P. Gaines. Indian retaliation was met by further escalation by the United States, and by March 1818 General Andrew Jackson was on the scene to put out the fire of Indian insurgency. With him was a fighting force of 4,800 troops, including 1,500 Creek Indians. Jackson lost no time in exploiting the rift between Seminole and Creek. He also clearly understood his mission and the desired outcome for the United States. From Fort Scott he swept into Spanish Florida on a scorched-earth offensive against the Florida Seminoles. The large village at Lake Micco-sukee was wiped out, the post at St. Marks attacked, and a move made against Bowlegs' Town on the west bank of the Suwannee River, all in one month's time. By May the general had turned west to capture the city of Pensacola. The confident Jackson proclaimed to the secretary of war that Cuba could be had with little further effort. Although this was not to be the case, the demonstration of American strength and Spanish weakness was clear. No Spanish retaliation came.

The Seminoles were pushed farther south in the peninsula, largely abandoning the productive agricultural regions of North Florida. Surely it was destined that this soil should become American. By 1821 Spanish Florida east of the Perdido River was transferred to the United States and was ruled by a territorial government. Now Florida was truly part of the slaveholding South. But what to do about the Seminoles who had escaped Jackson's surge? How many were there? Where did they live? And what to do about the Black Seminoles? Surely free black and black slave could not coexist in the same region. The Black Seminoles belonged to somebody and had to be returned. In any event, they did not, could not, belong to the Seminoles. That bond had to be broken.

Containment and Removal

From these attitudes developed the American policy of containment and removal. A head count was needed of all Florida Seminoles and their locations determined. This was done by Indian agents acting on the government's behalf, sometimes with the studied cooperation of the Indians themselves. Lists of Indian towns were produced, some based on information provided by Neamathla. Next, chiefs or headmen of each town had to be identified and contacted. They were to be asked to come to Moultrie Creek, a small tributary of the St. Johns River south of St. Augustine, to hear the terms of the American plan. This they did on September 6, 1823.

The terms were quite simple. First, the Indians were to give up claims to all of Florida, except lands designated for them by the government as a reservation. The Indians would agree to go on to the reservation. Once on the reservation, the government would protect the Indians against outsiders and would provide the reservation with $6,000 for tools and a stipend of $5,000 per year for twenty years. Because towns and families were expected to uproot to move to the reservation, the government would provide rations for one year and an additional $4,500. The reservation would be provided with an agent, interpreter, school, blacksmith, and gunsmith. All fugitive slaves making their way to Seminole territory were to be caught and returned.

On September 18, thirty-two Seminoles made their marks on the treaty, chief among them Neamathla, who was given a separate reservation near the Apalachicola as his reward. The Treaty of Moultrie Creek essentially was a formula for acculturation, and a flawed one at best. Benjamin Hawkins had tried many of the same elements among the Creek in the early part of the century, an effort that yielded the Creek War of 1814 as its most tangible result. With the Seminoles, the outcome would be no better. There were many things the U.S. government had not counted on or could not foresee.

Creating the reservation was itself a major difficulty. The Seminoles liked the fertile uplands near Tallahassee, but these were also most desired by the Americans. The farther south in the peninsula the boundaries were pushed, the poorer the maps and the more inadequate the geographical knowledge. Anchoring the southwest corner of the reservation at Tampa Bay had some positives, even though the area was not well known to the Americans. The harbor could provide a good access point for provisioning the reservation and the troops who were to guard its borders, and it would likewise provide a logical point of embarkation for Seminoles being shipped west to Indian Territory. However, at this time, fall 1823, the Seminoles were unaware of this eventuality.

More troubling difficulties were to come. Once the reservation boundaries had been determined, the Seminoles were expected in short order to move within them. One problem was that many Seminoles did not agree to do so, or felt like moving only reluctantly. Neamathla did not speak for them; besides, he was securely established in his own reservation well removed from the Seminole main. Much of the land was poor and not well known even to the Seminoles. They herded cattle; grew corn, beans, rice, and pumpkins; hunted, fished, and traveled the waterways and coasts of Florida in canoes; but they did not choose to live in swamps. But this is how much of the reservation appeared. How would they make a living here, even with government aid? How would they maintain their social ties?

A further sore point was the issue of fugitive slaves. Even Neamathla probably underrepresented the number of them among the Seminoles, in order to avoid widespread alarm among the Americans. Who was to determine the meaning of fugitive? Black Seminoles had become important to the Indians, as partners, as subordinates, as allies. Who was to say which of them was to go back? Their removal would surely upset the balance of labor in Seminole country. Such a thing would be a loss to the Seminoles. Even though the return of fugitive slaves had been agreed upon by the chiefs in the treaty, others stood to lose by such an agreement.

Red Sticks Fight Back

All these problems were brought on by the treaty provisions themselves. They could have been prevented had the Americans known the Seminoles better, and had they not tried to force upon them a structure of government and a way of life ultimately alien to the Indian way of doing things. But circumstances not foreseen by the government would prove to be the undoing of the entire scheme. These circumstances can be laid at Andrew Jackson's feet, for they were the unintended consequences of his strike against the Creeks in the so-called Creek War of 1814. It was in the Creek War that we see the first striking display of nativism among the Creeks, as the Red Sticks became followers of the Creek prophets.

By the early 1800s several strong forces were tearing apart Upper Creek society in middle Alabama. These Indians had had little exposure to the Spanish, British, and Americans over the years owing to their remote interior location, and they were buffered in their contact by the Lower Creeks along the Flint and Chattahoochee rivers. After the American Revolution, incessant pressure from settlers ruptured the frontier. The Creeks, in relatively short order, were thrown into direct contact with the Americans. Two factions developed among the Creeks. One group, popularly known as the loyals or friendlies, fell under the sway of the Americans, adopting their so-called progressive ways as peddled by Benjamin Hawkins, agent of the Creek Nation, and generally favoring American attempts to gain formal control of Creek territory. Some of these men became quite prosperous and ran plantations as respectable as any seen in this region of the South.

The second faction, less enamored with the prospects of acculturation, resisted the American presence and argued for a return to traditional Creek ways. They deeply resented losing Creek lands and castigated both the friendly Creeks and the Americans for their complicity. The words of the

Shawnee war chief Tecumseh met with ready acceptance among this faction. His fiery speech among them in 1811, exhorting the Creeks to throw aside the plow and loom and to take up the war club and scalping knife against the Americans, fueled their resistance and fanned them into action. Returning to the Ohio Valley, where he would ultimately meet his death, Tecumseh left in his wake a number of Creek prophets inspired by his teachings, men who experienced visions or divine communication with the Master of Breath. These men would become the spiritual core of the Red Sticks, red for the traditional color of war. Acting with divine guidance, the prophets led attacks on Creek towns loyal to the Hawkins plan, burning, pillaging, and destroying livestock, and they moved forward for a hoped-for decisive blow against the loyals and American militia stockaded at Fort Mims on the Alabama River. Capturing the fort, the Upper Creeks led by the wounded prophet Paddy Walch slaughtered some five hundred occupants within the fort's walls, including a number of women and children. From the American point of view, the conflict was no longer strictly Creek against Creek but had now escalated as an act of aggression against the United States. In rode Andrew Jackson.

The intrepid Indian fighter had a difficult time of it, but he finally pushed ahead to victory at the Battle of Horseshoe Bend. The war was declared over on August 8, 1814. The Red Stick resistance had been smashed, and twenty million more Creek acres became the property of the United States. But not all the Red Sticks lay dead in the waters of the Tallapoosa River. Some few made their way into Florida, first lurking within the swamps and creeks of the panhandle, then snaking their way south through the marshes and wetlands of the gulf coast. One such group was led by the prophet Francis, or Hillis Hadjo. Another group had with them a boy in his early teen years, a boy who was to be known in manhood as Osceola or Powell.

Jackson's offensive against the Seminoles in 1818 failed to dislodge them, most probably to his great disappointment. Some Red Sticks did filter back to Creek country after Jackson left the area, but others remained in their new home. The Florida Red Sticks, although never great in number, contributed a strong undercurrent of anti-American sentiment to the Seminole element. They had experienced firsthand the consequences of American intentions, and they knew how the American presence could divide native society. Yet they also knew that resistance was possible, at least for a time. Florida was larger than anyone knew, certainly much larger than the territory between the Coosa and Tallapoosa rivers. Maybe the Seminoles would be left alone, once the Americans appreciated the difficulties in rounding them up. Above all, land should not be given to the Americans, nor should the Seminoles agree to leave Florida.

It was the voices of these men, some Red Sticks, some Red-Stick influenced, that the Americans had not counted on to be heard among the Seminoles in the years following Moultrie Creek. These were years of mounting tensions, just as had happened among the Creeks in the years leading up to the Creek War. Some Seminoles saw the wisdom in complying with the American terms, which now included emigration following the 1832 Treaty of Paynes Landing. They began to divest themselves of their Florida holdings, mostly livestock, in preparation for the move to Indian Territory. Others continued to be outraged at the Moultrie Creek terms and were doubly defiant in the face of emigration. There was now a new generation of warriors among the Seminoles, men who had come of age under Spanish or American rule but were unproven in battle. To be a warrior required bold, fearless action. There were no longer other Indian nations that could be attacked or to make war upon, no prisoners to take, no scalps to be brandished high. For men like this, prospects of war with the Americans were not all that daunting. A plan was hatched.

Florida Aflame

Osceola and four warriors would lie in wait outside the palisade at Fort King and would kill Indian agent Wiley Thompson at the first opportunity. This was done on the afternoon of December 28, 1835. Osceola, it was later said by a captured Seminole, drew out Thompson's spirit. That was not all. The scalp was also removed from the lead-riddled body. Meanwhile, a warrior force led by Jumper, Alligator, and Micanopy, and including black allies led by Abraham, would ambush an advancing column of troops led by Major Francis Dade on the Fort King Road. As it happened, this also occurred on the twenty-eighth, although the intent had been for Osceola to join this ambush if possible. Upon Jumper's signal, and after the first shot by Micanopy, the Seminoles rose as one from behind palmetto and pine and blasted off a volley at Dade's men, just then winding their way through a narrow trail in the pine woods (fig 3.1). About one half of Dade's 108 soldiers dropped with these first shots. The rest, except for two, perished after a brief defense. That night in the Wahoo Swamp, Osceola rejoined the warriors for a victory celebration, featuring the scalps of Thompson and the others draped from atop a ten-foot-high pole.

3.1. Monuments mark where the dead of Dade's command fell in the Dade Battlefield State Historic Site. (Photograph courtesy of the Florida Park Service, Department of Environmental Protection.)

Thus ensued the seven-year-long Second Seminole War, the infamous war without a peace treaty, and one of the costliest Indian wars ever waged by the United States. The net result of the war in 1842 was fewer than three hundred Seminoles remaining in Florida where there once had been nearly five thousand and the deaths of more than fifteen hundred soldiers or citizens in service to the United States. This war focused the attention of American citizens on the Seminoles for the first time and created divided sympathies among them.

A number of Seminoles whose names are still known to many today—Osceola, Jumper, Wildcat, Sam Jones or Abiaka, and Micanopy—received media attention at the time and became figures of the popular imagination. Osceola in particular, painted on the verge of his death by George Catlin in 1838 at Fort Moultrie, delicate smile on his lips, high cheekbones, alluring eyes, white ostrich-plumed turban cocked slightly to the side, attracted much public sympathy, even being viewed as a native genius or a martyr for the cause of freedom. Indeed, Catlin's image is difficult to reconcile with the man who was Thompson's murderer, who returned from that deed, so later said Alligator, blood-smeared and with a warm scalp tucked beneath his girdle.

Yet the romantic cult of Osceola persists. The noted Danish author Karen Blixen, who later chose the pen name Isak Dinesen, wrote her first stories under the name Osceola. In Florida, a county he never set foot in and a national forest that never saw his camp bear his name, as do high schools and countless businesses. For a brief time perhaps the most feared of the Seminoles among the whites, he has now become a white man's Indian by virtue of appropriation. Some Indians seem ambivalent about him, and beyond his first campaign on the Withlacoochee River early in 1836, he never attracted many warriors to his command. Captured under a flag of truce in October 1837 by General Thomas S. Jesup (a circumstance thus partially accounting for the sympathies shown him), he was dead three months later from complications arising from malaria (fig. 3.2).

The war raged on for another four years. For many Americans, Florida was a long way away, a foreign land almost, certainly strange and mysterious. Of course, the tourist phenomenon was yet to develop (and would not until after the Civil War), and few knew Florida firsthand. This applied to the military as well, commanders and enlisted men alike. Accurate maps of the peninsula did not exist except for certain portions of the coast and lower St. Johns basin, where sugar plantations had been established. Many enlisted men were probably only barely familiar with the rest of the United States, as numbers of them were recent immigrants from the British Isles.

As a military campaign, the Second Seminole War was undistinguished. Of the seven military commanders who ultimately directed the Florida war, only one, Zachary Taylor, would emerge from the conflict with an unblemished reputation. Partly this was because he fought the only true pitched battle of the war, the Battle of Lake Okeechobee, and claimed victory. The efforts of the other commanders met with frustration, sometimes defeat, due to lack of communication, poor control over logistical necessities such as troop provisioning, and the difficulties of fighting an elusive foe under poor field conditions. The war itself began with the Dade ambush, although the fate of Dade's command was not known for some

3.2. The grave site of Osceola outside the walls of Fort Moultrie, South Carolina.

3.3. The Cove of the Withlacoochee consists of hardwood hammocks and uplands surrounded by wet prairies.

weeks. The news arrived at Fort Brooke only when two survivors crawled in after a journey of more than fifty miles. One was able to tell of their ordeal.

Meanwhile, on December 29, the day after the Dade battle and without knowledge of its outcome, General Duncan Clinch approached the Cove of the Withlacoochee from the east, intent on crossing the river and challenging the Seminoles in the center of their resistance. The so-called Cove of the Withlacoochee (fig. 3.3) is an area of about one hundred square miles formed in the bend of the gently north-flowing Withlacoochee River where it passes by and nearly joins with the lakes and wetlands of the Lake Tsala Apopka chain. Here the Seminoles began to gather in the months before the war. The area was unknown to the whites and was safely west of the Fort King Road, protected by the vast Wahoo Swamp and the wetlands of the Withlacoochee River. Crossing places were few and could be easily watched and guarded. A perfect place for a natural stronghold, the Cove also resembled the great "horseshoe bend" in the Tallapoosa River where the Creek resistors waited for Jackson's attack in the Creek War.

Ferrying over his men in an unlikely place in groups of six to eight in a leaky canoe, Clinch was able to get his troops across the river undetected but soon found himself under heavy fire from warriors led by Osceola and Alligator. The fight was spirited but brief before Clinch recrossed the river to safety with the loss of four regulars killed and twenty-five wounded. The Seminoles lost three, had five wounded, and saw two of Micanopy's Black

Seminoles killed, a loss that greatly upset him and dampened his interest in further conflict. Clinch retreated without clear victory as the Seminoles vanished among the cypress but held their ground. This much was certain: if you wanted to meet the Seminoles head on, or at least try to do so, you must come to the banks of the Withlacoochee.

The next to try was General Winfield Scott, who devised a three-prong offensive on the Cove consisting of two flank attacks and a push against the middle. This was standard tactics for dealing with a foe willing to mass against you on a battleground for face-to-face slaughter, as was the European tradition. But the Indians would play no such game, and the battlefield was miles of muck, swamp, and wilderness, not a tabletop. But before the plodding Scott could commence his campaign, on the scene an interloper appeared.

Hearing of the action and spoiling for a fight, General Edmund Gaines set sail from New Orleans with a fighting force of one thousand men. Intent on entering the thick of the Florida fray but acting without orders, Gaines advanced on the Cove in late February 1836. Scouring the bank for a crossing, as Clinch had done, and crossing briefly to find two of Clinch's dead disinterred by the Seminoles, Gaines recrossed the river to the east bank and picked his way north in the direction of an easier and more obvious crossing point. Here he found a canoe conveniently left for this purpose and, not surprisingly, a large group of Seminole warriors led by Osceola. Lieutenant James F. Izard fell mortally wounded with his first step into the river, and Gaines fell back under heavy fire to throw up a hasty log barricade later referred to as Camp or Fort Izard. From February 26 through March 5, Gaines and his men lay behind this barricade, three logs high, surrounded by the Seminoles and cut off from relief. Help eventually did come from Clinch and his base at Fort Drane but was not ordered by the enraged Scott. Unfortunately, Clinch's soldiers burst through the pine woods, rifles ablaze, at the very moment that the Seminoles had gathered at Izard for peace talks. This move freed Gaines but ended any hopes for a quick peace. The Seminoles again holed up in the Cove, where Scott would find them in his delayed three-prong offensive in late March. Scott found the Seminoles near the Clinch battleground and engaged them in an indecisive running battle in which the Seminoles gave way and in so doing enabled Scott to mire himself in the swamp. Scott pushed his way through the Cove, finding and burning some abandoned Seminole towns but failing to connect directly with the elusive Seminole foe. Blaming Gaines for prematurely engaging the Seminoles and thereby removing any element of surprise (although this was unlikely in any case), Scott brought Gaines before a court-martial inquiry.

Enter Andrew Jackson once again, now as president of the United States. The Cove must effectively be penetrated and the Seminoles decisively routed. For this task he chose territorial governor Richard Keith Call and a force of 2,500 men, some of them Tennessee Volunteers and some friendly Creeks whose tracking skills were valued. On November 21, 1836, Call found the Seminoles in the Wahoo Swamp at the south end of the Cove, lost his first man, Major David Moniac, a Creek Indian, as he tried to cross Battle Creek (fig. 3.4), and fought for several hours before withdrawing. Jackson had not found his man in Call and replaced him with General Thomas S. Jesup.

In Jesup's favor was a waning in the Seminole interest in prolonging the war. Open conflict had been under way for nearly one year, and weariness had set in, especially among Micanopy and his associates. They agreed to gather at Fort Brooke in early June 1837 for deportment west to Indian Territory. Jesup was elated. The war would end under his command. But this was not to happen, and in the next months Jesup would see his best plans unravel and a new plan of stealth and subterfuge emerge. It began when the seven hundred Seminoles with Micanopy camped outside Fort Brooke slipped away in the night under the persuasion of Osceola and the

3.4. Battle Creek, Sumter County, in the vicinity of the Battle of the Wahoo Swamp.

3.5. Archaeological excavations at the Okeechobee battlefield. (Photograph courtesy of the Archaeological and Historical Conservancy.)

medicine man Abiaka. Jesup, made to look the fool, vowed to take the Seminoles by any means.

On September 9, Coacoochee (Wildcat) was seized in Jesup's camp under a flag of truce. Osceola was captured in a similar ploy on October 27. Micanopy and his retinue were seized on December 14. Micanopy shipped west, Osceola died in prison at Fort Moultrie, and Wildcat escaped to join with Abiaka's band to fight again. Still, Jesup had struck a strong but ignoble blow against the Seminole leadership. By the time he stepped down as commander in May 1838, 1,978 Seminoles had been deported, another four hundred or so killed. This included the dead from the Battle of Okeechobee, fought on the north rim of the lake on Christmas Day, 1837.

Archaeologists' metal detectors and careful test excavations have located physical remains of the battle, and the site is now listed in the National Register of Historic Places (fig. 3.5). Troops led by Colonel Zachary Taylor faced a battle line held by Alligator's warriors at the center, those of Sam Jones and the Prophet Otulke-thloco on the right, and Wildcat's men on the left. Altogether, 480 Seminoles faced 1,032 soldiers in the pitched fight, and when their line broke, Taylor, alone among army leaders during the war, was able to claim victory. No glory reflected on his commander, Jesup, and Taylor wound up with a promotion to Brigadier General. As such, he was next in line to assume command after Jesup's resignation.

Despite Jesup's relative success in ridding Florida of the Seminoles, a thousand remained for Taylor to contend with. As an added challenge to the U.S. effort, bands of Seminoles began filtering back north and were roaming the territory between the Apalachicola and Suwannee rivers and their old heartland around the Alachua savanna and other points in Central Florida. Powerful bands had formed in the Big Cypress, as we will see in chapter 4, under the leadership of Billy Bowlegs, Sam Jones, and the renegade Creek Prophet Otulke-thloco. Faced with the possibility that the Seminoles would not be dislodged from Florida and may even again gain control over the territory, Taylor devised a twofold strategy. North of the Withlacoochee River, the land would be divided into squares twenty miles on a side, with a fort in the middle. Regular military patrols of the squares would sweep them clean of Seminoles and thus prevent their takeover of Central and North Florida.

The Big Cypress Swamp was another matter. Perhaps the Seminoles there could be allowed to remain. The terrain was harsh, not suitable for the type of farming that made the North Florida lands so desirable. General Alexander Macomb arrived in May 1839 to negotiate a deal. Seminoles who signed his pact would be allowed to remain on 6,700 acres in the Big Cypress. But this deal did not set well with the more aggressive Florida settlers or with the more hardened Seminole resisters. The attack by Chakaika and Hospetarke on Colonel William S. Harney's camp and the Caloosahatchee trading post in July 1839, as discussed in chapter 4, was a dramatic rejection of the Macomb pact. Taylor saw his hopes for the conquest of the Seminoles vanish, and he was relieved from command by General Walker Armistead.

Armistead failed to improve on Taylor's figures, however, and shipped seven hundred Seminoles west (including Black Seminoles) compared to Taylor's eight hundred Indians and four hundred blacks. Nonetheless, Seminole strength and numbers were diminished.

By June 1841, when Colonel William Jenkins Worth assumed command of the Florida regulars, hard pockets of resistance still existed in the Big Cypress and in the former stronghold in the Cove of the Withlacoochee. The Indians in these areas—led by Bowlegs, Sam Jones, the Prophet, and the Creek fugitive Octiarche—would not budge. But Osceola was long dead, now just a memory. Micanopy and Alligator were gone. Even the wily Coacoochee or Wildcat, whose supernatural escape from behind bars at Fort Marion inspired his followers in 1837, became a captive in June and was shipped west. Still Worth persisted. Soldiers were sent into the remote swamps to look for Indian signs, to follow every trail. All fields, all crops, all houses were to be burned. At one camp on a hammock island in the Cove, the soldiers reported destroying 12,000 pounds of jerked beef, left on the shore by fleeing Indians. This suggests that remaining herds were being slaughtered in haste to prepare for life on the run. No doubt the Seminoles were suffering under Worth's squeeze.

By April 1842 only three hundred Seminoles remained. Over the seven years of the war, 4,420 Seminoles had been captured and deported to Indian Territory. Countless others, numbering at least in the several hundreds, lay dead and buried in Florida soil. The Fort Brooke cemetery alone contained the remains of nearly forty Seminole men, women, and children who died of disease awaiting deportation. Warriors had been killed in action at Izard, the Battle of the Withlacoochee, Scott's engagement, the Wahoo Swamp, the Fort Foster crossing on the Hillsborough River, the Battle of Okeechobee, and in other skirmishes and isolated encounters. Some were hastily buried in the middens or refuse piles of Florida's prehistoric Indians, such as the Seminole placed in a shallow grave in a Hialeah midden in Dade County. Here were found wedged between two trees with fragmentary skeletal remains such artifacts as a single-ball bullet mold made of soapstone, military uniform buttons, remnants of a .36-caliber Kentucky rifle, glass beads, a silver cone and bangle (fig. 3.6), and a portion of a glass mirror.

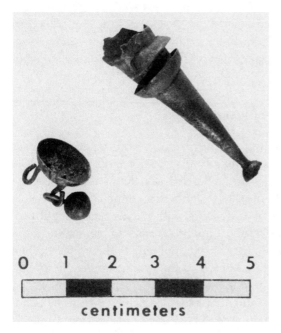

0 1 2 3 4 5

centimeters

3.6. Silver earring and bangle from the Seminole burial in the Hialeah midden, Dade County, dating to the era of the Second Seminole War. (Photograph courtesy of the Anthropology Department, Florida Museum of Natural History, FLMNH Cat. No. 92651.)

The hardships of the Second Seminole War impressed themselves into the Seminole cultural memory, where they have been preserved in traditional beliefs and practices involving war magic. Some men were said to have possessed supernatural power. These men were not necessarily the chief or leading warriors, but a wise war leader would have one of these men among his band. They could make tracks and trails invisible, ruin the nose of a bloodhound, and change into a bear and run swiftly to safety with children on their back. The sorcerers could make themselves invisible or impervious to pain or the effects of bullets. Coacoochee escaped from Fort Marion in St. Augustine in 1837 by shrinking his body and the bodies of his twenty followers to fit between the cell bars and by using magic to put the guards to sleep.

Magic songs were used to protect the Seminoles when they parleyed with the soldiers. Many objects in the Seminole medicine bundles are meant to give power in war, particularly by casting spells over the soldiers or by shielding the people from harm. Clearly the Seminoles used everything in their power to keep the military at bay, but the United States was just as determined in its will to remove the Indians. But seven years of conflict was a long time for both sides. The regular army saw 1,466 deaths, 74 of them officers. Every regiment served in Florida, making this one of the costliest Indian wars ever waged by the United States. The net result was a truce, not a treaty, and Billy Bowlegs, Sam Jones, and their bands were allowed to inhabit the remote areas of the Big Cypress Swamp. This they did in relative peace and obscurity for another seven years. But by 1849, whites were encroaching on lands that had previously been considered to be completely undesirable.

Conflicts Unresolved: The Billy Bowlegs War

It seemed certain to be only a matter of time before white settlement reached every corner of the state. In July 1849, four warriors fired into the Kennedy and Darling trading store on Peace Creek, killing Captain George Payne and Dempsey Whiddon as they sat down to dinner. They may have been disgruntled about previous dealings with Payne, who bought produce, venison, and beeswax from the Indians for sale in New York, or the provocation may have been for reasons known only to themselves. When the Kennedy and Darling store burned to the ground under the Indian torch, fear and panic spread among the white settlers of the region.

A new series of forts was built across the peninsula to keep the Seminoles contained in the south. In 1850, three other warriors from Chipco's band captured and killed a boy who had been sent on a farm errand. The public demanded revenge; newspaper editorials called for a bounty of $1,000 placed on the head of every warrior captured, five hundred dollars for every woman and child. But the United States was not eager to be dragged into another fight with the Seminoles. The army had, understandably, lost its taste for fighting an Indian war in Florida. Efforts were made to entice the Indians out peacefully. Billy Bowlegs was taken to Washington to see for himself the size of the government that hoped to control him, but to no avail. Money was offered, but Bowlegs would not leave Florida.

The secretary of war, Jefferson Davis, had had enough. Floridians were screaming for action. Davis made it illegal to trade with the Seminoles and ordered the survey of lands within their Big Cypress reservation. In December 1855, the military survey crew led by Lieutenant George Hartsuff burst into Billy Bowlegs' empty camp, vandalizing it and allegedly destroying his prized banana plants. On December 18, Hartsuff's ten men were fired on by Billy Bowlegs and his thirty warriors. Four dropped dead and four were wounded. Thus began the Third Seminole War, also known as the Billy Bowlegs War.

It took two years for the combined army, militia, and volunteer force to find Billy Bowlegs, and this only after sending in ragtag volunteers on board customized shallow draft vessels. On November 19, 1857, the boat troops found and burned Bowlegs' camp, consisting of some fifty dwellings, torched his fields, and took large quantities of corn and rice and some oxen. Bowlegs knew this was the end of his way of life and decided to go west. Terms were reached, and on May 4, 1858, Billy Bowlegs and 164 Seminoles saw Florida for the last time and set sail for the new two-million-acre Seminole reservation in Indian Territory.

A Spirit Rekindled

Sam Jones, by now nearly one hundred years old, never came in and stayed on deep in the Everglades with a small band of warriors. Other bands were scattered throughout the Big Cypress and Everglades regions, around the rim of Lake Okeechobee and north through the Kissimmee River valley. After the exodus of Bowlegs and his band, fewer than two hundred Seminoles remained in Florida. These Indians withdrew from all willing contact with whites and existed for twenty years in isolation. These two hundred were the cultural and biological Mayflower for the Seminoles and Miccosukees of today. It was through these Indians that cultural traditions many hundreds of years old were carried forward and changed to fit the socially and geographically isolated conditions of the South Florida swamps. It was through them that practices and beliefs of the ancestral Creeks and nameless cultures of the archaeological record ancestral to the Creeks were kept alive. It may be that the stressful conditions of the war years even intensified and distilled these traditions, making them stronger among the Seminoles than otherwise may have been the case.

It would seem to go against common sense to say that the trauma of the Seminole wars may have in fact revitalized Seminole culture. Certainly the death and suffering of individuals cannot be construed as anything positive. But despite the many hardships brought on by the long years of hostilities, the Seminoles kept their ancient traditions alive. More than this, they added new elements, some with the purpose of helping them deal with the white man and his ways. The Seminole Indians visited by Clay MacCauley in 1881 were far diminished in number compared to pre-1835 levels but were not diminished in religious or spiritual beliefs.

How did the Seminoles manage to keep the core of their culture alive, even as they were being relentlessly assailed by the military? One answer can be found with the prophets. The activities of several prophets among the Seminoles have been documented historically. One of them, Otulke-thloco, had moved to Florida after the Creek War of 1836 and had accomplished this, he claimed, by breaking free from the irons that bound his hands and feet. His talents largely were in the area of divination. If an Indian was suspected of intending to emigrate, Otulke-thloco would be called in to get to the bottom of the matter. Dances and prayers were used to make contact with the Great Spirit. At the right time, the Prophet would blow through a pipe on to the palm of the distressed person and then would carefully scrutinize the palm for a reading of that person's intent. An intent to emigrate or evidence of contact with the white man could result in death. The Prophet's power was great but was ultimately rejected when it fell short of his claims. Nonetheless, at its height, Seminoles encamped at Fort Brooke preparing to emigrate were said to have held sacred dances at night to ward off the Prophet's malevolence, which, apparently, could extend great distances from his camp in the Big Cypress. Despite his eventual downfall, the Prophet's activities served to focus attention on the Great Spirit and reinforced the specific ritual means, including fires, prayers, and medicines, that allowed communication with the supreme being.

Osceola and his small band of loyal Red Sticks also may have played a role in keeping the teachings of Tecumseh alive, to "throw off the plow and the loom," to reject the white man's ways. Although not actually recognized as a prophet, Osceola did rely on spiritual power to direct his actions. A companion later said that Osceola lay in wait outside the walls of Fort King until he drew out the spirit of Indian agent Wiley Thompson and, having done this, shot him dead.

The military scouting party that discovered Osceola's abandoned camp deep in the Withlacoochee River swamp in April 1837 found it to be a squareground, a typical town plan for the Creeks and early Seminoles but perhaps less popular among them since Cowkeeper's time. Was this an attempt by Osceola to connect his efforts with Creek and Seminole tradition? The location of Osceola's site, in the great bend of the Withlacoochee River, is similar to the location of Tohopeka, in the bend of the Tallapoosa River, where the Red Sticks made their last stand against Andrew Jackson. Years before, William Bartram observed that the Creeks favored such locations for their villages because they were secure from sudden invasion. Did Osceola think of himself as a bearer of Red Stick tradition? Very near the Osceola camp, known as Powell's Town to the soldiers (because Osceola was often referred to as Powell, the name of his white father), hidden in a thick oak scrub, is a burial mound belonging to the earlier prehistoric Indians of the area. In excavations of that mound in the 1980s, a single blue faceted glass bead, unmistakably Seminole, was found just below the present ground surface. Did Osceola know of the mound? Was it important to him to have his village located nearby, perhaps as a way of gaining spiritual strength? These questions, however compelling, must go without answers. History simply does not tell us enough about Osceola to know.

But the archaeological record of Seminole occupation in the Cove or great bend of the Withlacoochee during Osceola's time brings questions and answers of its own. Excavations at Powell's Town revealed that the material culture of the camp was sparse, nearly ascetic. Lead shot, sherds of broken bottle glass and pottery, peach pits, fragmentary cow bones, and a bridle bit are all that mark the location of the site. Nearby, a three-legged cast-iron cook pot was found (fig. 3.7). Where are the glass beads and the many fragments of English transfer-print, shell-edged, and banded-pearlware ceramics that are typically found in Creek and Seminole sites dating to this period?

To the south of Powell's Town, beyond the wetlands and below one lobe of Lake Tsala Apopka, lies the remains of a much larger Seminole village. Spread across the gentle sandy swales of an orange grove and in the backyards of a small rural subdivision, just below the modern ground surface, are pottery sherds, glass bottle fragments, rusted iron tools, and other ob-

3.7. The cast-iron cook pot found in the archaeological survey of the Powell's Town site, Osceola's Second Seminole War village in the Cove of the Withlacoochee.

jects once belonging to Seminole Indian families (fig. 3.8). Military buttons found in excavations place occupation at the site during the period of the Second Seminole War. But again, where are the European ceramics? None have been found in systematic surface collections and test excavations of the village. Yet such ceramics are telltale archaeological signatures of Creek and Seminole sites of the period just prior to the war.

True, their absence can be accounted for in several plausible ways. Perhaps as villages and households picked up and moved to more remote areas in the early months of the war the cumbersome ceramics were simply left behind. And once cut off from regular sources of supply at Fort King and other trading outposts, perhaps dwindling supplies could not be replaced. But why ceramics and not glass bottles? And certainly if it was just a matter of supply or inconvenience, some ceramics would be found at the Seminole war-period village sites, perhaps just in diminished numbers. Instead, their complete absence suggests that another explanation is worth considering. If the possession of these ceramics had become symbols of acculturation among the Creeks and Seminoles, symbols of success and prestige, then their rejection would likewise become a powerful statement against the American influence. Indeed, few of these ceramics have been recovered archaeologically from Tohopeka. A rejection of the ceramics associated with the dominant society becomes part of the revival of traditional aboriginal society, or what anthropologists call a nativistic movement. Nativism, if it existed among the early Seminole resisters gathered in the Cove of the Withlacoochee, meant not only rejecting the values of the society that was oppressing them but also rekindling traditional values of what it meant to be Indian.

The Green Corn Dance was held throughout Seminole country during the Second Seminole War. Billy Bowlegs hosted at least one dance in the Big Cypress. Others may have been held repeatedly in the swamps near Lake Panasoffkee, just across the river from the Cove of the Withlacoochee, according to the testimony of captured Black Seminoles. Intriguing but incomplete archaeological evidence from the Withlacoochee area suggests

3.8. Archaeological excavations at the Newman's Garden site, Citrus County, reveal the remains of a structure probably occupied by a Seminole family in the early years of the Second Seminole War.

3.9. A Seminole dance, 1838, drawn by Hamilton Wilcox Merrill outside Fort Butler on the St. Johns River. (Reproduced with the permission of the Florida Anthropological Society and the Huntington Library, San Marino, California.)

that a special pottery vessel may have been made and broken as part of the ceremony, which took place in a layer of clean sand placed to cover a low mound of an earlier prehistoric Indian midden. Other types of dances and ceremonies took place after victories or when the warriors returned home unharmed. Scalps were taken and brandished, then attached to a pole in the center of the dance ground. Guns were fired into the air amidst chants. Masks must have figured in some of the dances, based on what the soldiers found when they entered Snake Warriors Island. On April 2, 1836, troops entered the abandoned Black Seminole town of Peliklakaha in Central

Florida and found there a ball stick used in the ball game portion of the Green Corn Dance, a flute, and a turtle shell filled with palmetto seeds to be worn as a dance rattle.

In November or December 1838 in a small clearing on the west bank of the St. Johns River near present-day Astor, eleven Seminole warriors locked arms in a circle, dancing around a low central fire. Sprawled around them a woman and several children watched as the men, some stripped to breechclouts, others wearing appliqued long shirts and feathered headbands, danced and sang (fig. 3.9). Nearby sat a twenty-four-year-old West Point–trained lieutenant, Hamilton Wilcox Merrill, silently sketching the scene that lay before him. History has not recorded Merrill's thoughts on what he saw, nor do we know who these Seminoles were, why they were there, or the reason for their dance. Yet Merrill captured this scene because he knew, as did all who met the Seminoles during this period, that their resistance was more than determined, it was spirited.

→ 4 ←

Big Water, Grass River

↑ ↑ ↑ ↑ ↑ ↑ ↑ ↑ ↑ ↑ ↑ ↑ ↑

The Everglades was not meant to be a home for human beings, so said Marjory Stoneman Douglas, late matriarch defender of the Everglades and author of the environmental classic *The Everglades: River of Grass,* published in 1947. Before her, writing in 1929, the noted botanist John Kunkel Small offered the same blunt sentiments. Doubtless thousands of motorists would agree with them as they speed back and forth across the Tamiami Trail or the newer Alligator Alley on their way to or from paradise. With the air-conditioning at full blast and safely encased in metal, glass, and plastic, it might be possible to think of the Everglades as something less than hostile to human existence, for those inclined in the least to contemplate such things. To think this way would be a mistake. Before the opening of the Tamiami Trail in 1928, the Glades were rarely traversed from coast to coast, and when done it was by expeditions of adventurers eager to kill trophy gators and panthers and record their exploits.

In 1892, one of the first attempts to cross the Everglades by whites nearly ended in tragedy, had it not been for the sudden lucky appearance of a Seminole who pointed the weary, saw-grass-bloodied group toward the headwaters of the Miami River. Thus ended the interest of railroad magnate Henry Flagler in extending the tracks of the Florida Coast and Gulf Railway Company through this great swamp. To be fair, not all Seminoles have taken to the Everglades. In 1933, George Jones of the Oklahoma Seminoles visited the area only long enough to remark to a local paper, "Jackson and his men drove my people from Florida at the point of the bayonet, and if we ever go back it'll be the same way." Old Chipco, a Florida Seminole, is reported to have said upon his return to the Lake Wales Ridge in the 1870s after twenty years in the south, "me get tired wading water all the time. Me come back to the sand hills and lakes."

Humans have come late to Pahayokee or Piokee, "river of grass," although there was prehistoric occupation of the eastern rock ridge almost

10,000 years ago. Archaeological sites at Cutler Ridge and Weston Pond have yielded Bolen-type stone projectile points from solution holes in the rock and suggest a hunting lifestyle similar to the North Florida Indians of that time. The Everglades wetlands had yet to form. Instead, savanna vegetation covered interior South Florida. Prehistoric forays deeper into the savanna at this early date were probably tentative at best, and even the black dirt middens accumulated many millennia later by prehistoric fishers, gatherers, and hunters on the scattered tree islands in the Everglades are small and unimpressive by Florida standards. The anthropologist John Goggin saw the Everglades as central to prehistoric cultures in South Florida, not because it was a desirable place to live, but because its inaccessibility kept them apart. Yet this vast watery wilderness—harsh, remote, unforgiving—was home to the ancestors of today's Seminoles and Miccosukees and is at the core of how they think of themselves as a people.

To understand the dynamic interaction between culture and environment in South Florida, one can begin by considering the natural environment. In terms of cultural geography, South Florida can be divided into five areas, ecologically inseparable, yet each unique in what it could offer to the Seminole way of life (fig. 4.1).

The first area is the Everglades itself, a broad 5,000-square-mile sloping shelf south of Lake Okeechobee consisting of marine limestones formed from shallow sea deposits between one and ten million years ago. Wave action from the ancient waters of the Atlantic Ocean and Gulf of Mexico caused the sea bottom to slope to the southeast and southwest. With the lowering of sea level near the end of the Pleistocene Ice Age, when the ice caps made their final expansion, the platform became raised slightly above sea level. Between 5,000 and 7,000 years ago, as sea levels rose, the waters of Lake Okeechobee began flowing across its surface toward the sea. Through time a veneer of muck covered the bare rock, enough to support extensive stands of saw grass. Not a true grass, this sedge sometimes grows ten feet tall and is set with sharp teeth on its edges, capable of tearing clothes from flesh and leaving the flesh itself with deep, painful wounds. Despite the grass, the flow to the sea continues.

Although virtually imperceptible to an observer on the ground, the slow movement of water through the Glades is easily appreciated from the air through the remarkable aerial photography of recent years. In 1930 the Florida Geological Survey considered the Everglades to contain three million acres. But this was just as Big Sugar began gobbling up the northern portion south of Lake Okeechobee and before the westward expansion of Miami and Fort Lauderdale devoured the eastern edge. Now, far fewer

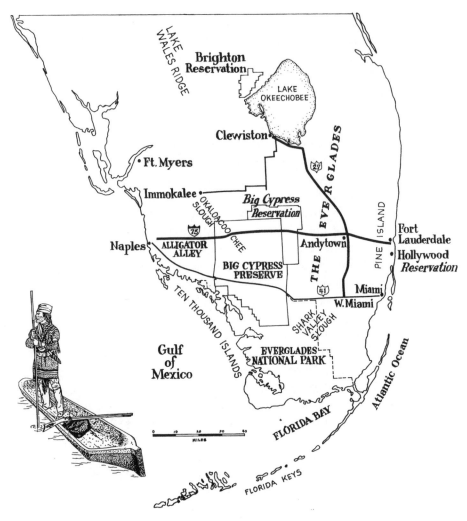

4.1. Natural and cultural areas of South Florida. (Drawn by Theodore Morris and reproduced with the author's permission.)

acres are preserved by Everglades National Park, considered by many to be the most endangered U.S. park.

Anchored in this river of grass are limestone outcrops with enough soil and adequate drainage to support tree growth. On these tree islands, or hammocks, grow palms, palmettos, slash pines, the gumbo-limbo, and strangler fig. If humans were to live in the Everglades, it would have to be on these islands, and it is here that bands of Seminoles came as early as the 1840s. Fifty years later, when Seminole families were occasionally encountered on these hammock islands by adventurers, naturalists, government agents, or anthropologists it was often at the point of a gun. To the outside world, Seminole life in the Everglades was a closely guarded secret. As late as 1915, some Seminole children in these island camps had yet to see a white man.

The Bad Country

No less remote is the Big Cypress Swamp, so named because of the many cypress trees that form dense stands in the low-lying landscape. Like the adjacent Everglades, Big Cypress is perched on a slanting rock platform that allows only slow movement of water to the south and southwest through networks of strands, sloughs, and prairies. Intense summer rains averaging sixty inches per year fill the basin during the wet season from June to October as waters from the Kissimmee valley and Okeechobee collect for their southward flow. As in the Everglades, plant and animal life in the Big Cypress beats to the pulse of the wet and dry seasons.

Prehistoric Florida Indians found it worth their while to hunt and fish in the Big Cypress. The numerous black dirt middens found on the Big Cypress tree islands tell of their success in the food quest. Rather than living in the swamp year-round, these aboriginal cultures probably figured out the best time to most easily gather the largest number of fish and turtles and hunt mammals such as deer, perhaps returning to their large shell midden villages on the mangrove coast of the Ten Thousand Islands for the rest of the year. Some of the larger midden sites are the remains of camps occupied either for longer periods during the year or more frequently through the years than others.

Archaeologists are uncertain of when the Big Cypress was first inhabited in prehistory or for how long, because although the middens contain well-preserved remains of the animal species taken for food, artifacts diagnostic of specific time periods or charcoal from cooking fires usable for radiocarbon dating are rarer finds. Most of the known radiocarbon dates document prehistoric occupation after about A.D. 900, although it is likely that the area was regularly inhabited after A.D. 500.

The eastern half of the Big Cypress was used by people belonging to an archaeological culture extending from Cape Sable north to Biscayne Bay and south through the Florida Keys, to judge from Key Largo–type pottery present, while peoples of the western half belonged to a culture centered in the Ten Thousand Islands, where Gordon Pass pottery is found. Archaeologists once equated these two archaeological subdivisions with the Calusa

and Tequesta tribes known in the historic period, although this nomenclature has recently fallen from favor. Regardless of the small cultural differences reflected in the pottery types, neither group fared well in the period
after initial European contact, and archaeological sites dating after the early
sixteenth century are rare. The same can be said for the Everglades.

The Seminoles often used these same tree islands for their camps, taking
advantage of the slightly higher elevation built up by the extra layers of soil
resulting from the earlier prehistoric occupations. This soil was also fertile
enough to grow gardens of corn, squash, melons, and peas. In the 1890s,
naturalist Charles Cory of Chicago's Field Museum asked Old Charlie and
Robert Osceola about these prehistoric mounds, to be told "Injuns all dead
. . . Injuns came in canoe, eat oysters, play ball." Make no mistake, Cory was
further told, those Indians were not Seminoles.

The Big Cypress failed to impress white observers, leaving many with
the opinion that it was one of the dreariest places on earth, a vast desolate
wilderness of waste and water. "Bad country" is how even the most objective referred to it. Impassable in the wet season except by canoe, the Big
Cypress was protected all year by the difficult passage through the Oka-
loacoochee Slough, part of a sixty-mile-long bog guarding the northwest-
ern access to the swamp. Above the slough northwest toward Fort Myers
were pine, palmetto, and cabbage palm flatwoods and scrub, always hot
but reasonably dry. Below the slough were the wet prairies, swamps, and
strands of the Big Cypress. From the Second Seminole War journal of C. R.
Gates comes this account of December 7, 1841, of the Eight Regiment crossing the slough in the hope of attacking Waxey Hadjo's village: "water knee
deep, and boggy; three mules bogged; Captain Scriven's pack thrown into
the water, lost his sugar and bread."

It was in the Big Cypress that the heart and soul of the Seminole resistance sought refuge in the closing years of the Second Seminole War, when
Billy Bowlegs, Sam Jones (Abiaka), the Prophet, Waxey Hadjo, and Chitto-
Tustenuggee, "desperate characters" in the words of the U.S. military,
brought their people to the swamp's pine islands in 1840 to rebuild a base
of power. Sam Jones may have been here as early as 1828, perhaps in antici-
pation of the hostilities that were to come. Neatly pruned orange groves
now grow where once the Eighth Regiment prepared to cross the Oka-
loacoochee Slough in pursuit of the intransigent Seminoles. Most of the
slough itself lies beyond the boundaries of the Big Cypress National Preserve, established by Congress in 1974 to protect what remained of the
Everglades watershed. On the Indian side, the location of the Big Cypress

Seminole Indian Reservation near the north end of the swamp preserves the association between the tribe and this significant historical and cultural area.

A third region of South Florida of some importance to the Seminole story is the Ten Thousand Islands and mangrove coast of the Everglades. Here rise the huge shell mounds of nameless prehistoric cultures that once occupied what must have been one of the most densely inhabited regions of aboriginal Florida. Beginning at Cape Romano near Marco, where the eccentric Frank Hamilton Cushing found the delicately carved Marco cat in the muck of a collapsed ceremonial water court, and extending through a string of broken islands and mangrove fringe to the Shark River north of Cape Sable, the rich waters of the River of Grass nourish one of the most biologically abundant food chains in the world. The dissected waterways feeding into the Gulf of Mexico and Florida Bay abound in oysters, clams, shrimp, countless fish, alligators, bird life, and mammals such as raccoons and otters. An ideal location for the Indian way of life, so thought Charles Torrey Simpson and John C. Gifford, leading naturalists of their day, in writing their endorsements of the 99,200-acre Seminole Indian reservation established by the State of Florida in 1917 in this area.

But the Seminoles were not like the prehistoric ancestors of the Calusa and Tequesta Indians. Unappreciated by the naturalists and others impressed by the natural bounty of the Florida subtropics was the fact that the Seminoles were not and never had been an aquatic culture. This had been the domain of the so-called Spanish Indians, a mixed group of Calusa, Seminole, and Cuban outcasts led by the notorious Chakaika, but the extent to which Seminole families actually settled within the reservation boundaries is a matter of some contention because of the eventual displacement caused by the creation of Everglades National Park.

The major importance of this coastal area to the Seminoles was not as a place to live, for few archaeological sites linked to the Seminoles have been found in comprehensive surveys. Rather, it was in this area that Indian and white eventually were to interact on friendly terms, as the reclusive Seminoles came out late in the 1800s to trade deerskins and alligator hides at stores established by Smallwood, Storter, and others on Chokoloskee Island. It was also a place to hunt. In 1892, when the Ingraham expedition passed through a Seminole village in the eastern Everglades twenty-five miles northwest of Miami, the men of the village were hunting at Chokoloskee sixty-five miles away.

Life on the Everglades Fringe

Bands of Seminoles also settled above the northwest rim of Lake Okee-chobee, an area of prairie, pine flatwoods, and oak-cabbage palm hammocks interspersed with wetland sloughs and swamps. Although this area is drier than the Big Cypress or the Everglades, the rains are heavy and hard here and often too much for the poorly drained soils, resulting in standing water covering many areas during the wet season. In October 1948, 95 percent of Brighton Reservation's 36,000 acres were under water due to heavy rains, and the Red Cross set up shelters for one hundred evacuees. Particularly important to these Seminoles were the grassy expanses of the dry prairies and the open cabbage palm savannas that made good natural pastures for cattle. To the east were the Blue Cypress Swamps of the St. Johns Marsh, an area that these Okeechobee Seminoles found attractive for settlement. From their camps along Cow Creek or deep in the marsh, Seminole bands would occasionally make their way through the pine and palmetto flatwoods to the trading post on the coast near Fort Pierce.

Well to the south, and now all but swallowed up by the sprawling western suburbs of Fort Lauderdale and Hollywood in today's Broward County, there exists a generally westward trending string of sand islands. These relict dunes formed from sand blown from Pleistocene beaches rise from the Everglades almost like islands in the sea and form the most substantial toehold for human populations in the eastern Everglades. The Seminoles settled here in the 1820s, and by the 1840s the islands enter the historical record with names such as Sam Jones Island, Chittos Island, Prophets Island, Council Island, and the Pine Island Ridge.

Among these islands, Pine Island Ridge was to achieve particular importance to Seminole culture. The ridge, actually a group of six smaller islands once separated by wet prairie sloughs and channels, rises in places twenty-nine feet above sea level. Although drainage and intensive development have made the true shape of the ridge virtually undetectable in modern aerial photographs, earlier maps reveal a contorted landscape shaped by the agents of wind and water. Its deep sandy soils gave stands of oaks and pines a chance to grow in an area otherwise dominated by muck, and the understory of *Zamia* or coontie provided an extra attraction to the first bands of Seminole settlers who learned how to pound its starchy roots into flour.

This was the mosaic of environments that confronted the Seminoles on their move into South Florida. All of them driven by the flow of water and all more or less inhospitable to the human presence, the subtropical environments of South Florida were an important stimulus for new developments in Seminole culture nevertheless. The dispersed pattern of settlement that existed in earlier Creek and Seminole society as but one aspect of a system based on central towns now became the norm. Although there were important social reasons why this was so, as we have already seen, the fact remains that the South Florida landscape, with the notable exception of the Pine Island complex, provided few opportunities for nucleated settlement. Lacking both large-scale agriculture and a natural environment in which food resources were abundant and stationary, the Seminoles had but little choice to live a mobile existence in camps scattered throughout the tree islands of the South Florida swamps.

In South Florida the Seminoles introduced their distinctive open-air, palmetto-thatched house, or *chickee* (from the Mikasuki word *ciki*, meaning "house"). It is easy to think of the chickee as a logical adaptation to the heat of South Florida, especially in the days when home cooling depended solely on breeze and shade. However, the specific historical origins of the Seminole chickee are not known. Some have suggested that the chickee resulted from contact between the Seminoles and cultures of the Caribbean, where similar dwellings exist. Others say that the chickee style was brought by those few Calusa remnants absorbed by the South Florida Seminoles, based on the assumption that this house had been developed years earlier by this indigenous Florida tribe. I think the answer lies within Seminole culture itself. They always had the open-air, pole-and-thatch construction technique, used for storage areas attached to their main dwellings. Bartram gives us a description of one such storage structure from the town of Cuscowilla in North Florida in 1775: "[T]he end next the dwelling house is open on three sides, supported by posts or pillars. It has an open loft or platform, the ascent to which is by a portable stair or ladder."

When the Seminoles moved south in the 1820s, they took this construction technique with them and left behind the four-walled log or board cabin style. Military descriptions of Seminole villages, as few as they are, indicate that cabins, not chickees, were built by Seminoles in North and Central Florida during the years of the Second Seminole War, 1835–1842. The first depiction of a chickee shows the settlement of Sam Jones in a watercolor by Seth Eastman, of an unknown South Florida location in the early 1840s and a structure that is clearly the prototype of the modern Seminole chickee (fig. 4.2). Eastman, an artist and West Point man, was stationed in Florida in 1840–1841 and may have been part of the patrol that came upon Jones's camp after its abandonment.

Further refinements in chickee architecture must have occurred through

4.2. Seth Eastman's watercolor depiction of the Sam Jones camp. Note the coontie log and pestle in the foreground and the lack of raised floors in the dwellings. (Photograph courtesy of the Peabody Museum, Harvard University. Photograph by Hillelburger.)

the 1840s up to the 1870s, resulting in the structures of a most excellent kind noted by Clay MacCauley in his visit to the camp of I-ful-lo-ha-tco or Charlie Osceola in the Bad Country on the edge of the Big Cypress in October 1880 (fig. 4.3). Charlie Osceola's house consisted of a sixteen-by-nine-foot platform raised three feet from the ground covered with a palmetto-thatched roof. The steeply pitched roof was held aloft by eight upright palmetto logs, their bases firmly buried in the ground, which also provided support for the raised platform and the rafters. Easy access to the rafters eliminated the need for storage space on the floor.

Because Charlie Osceola was not home, MacCauley could prowl the camp at his leisure. Peering up to the rafters, MacCauley spotted a pile of dressed buckskins, an old rifle, and a shot flask and powder horn. Nearby hung a bag of corn and next to it a sack of clothing.

The floor of split palmetto logs rested on beams lashed by rope to the posts. The rafters and ridge pole were secured in a similar fashion. No nails were used. Most remarkable was the technique of thatching the roof, a skill that involved the careful interweaving of the inner palmetto fronds to achieve waterproofing (fig. 4.4). Extra layers of fronds were heaped on the outer surface of the roof to protect the woven inner surface and were held in place by pairs of bound logs straddling the ridge pole. MacCauley could not think of a house better suited for the environment and remarked that the elevated platform was safely above the frequently rising water that would drown the dry land of the camp.

Clay MacCauley believed that I-ful-lo-ha-tco's house was typical of all Seminole houses throughout the "Seminole district," but some variation almost certainly existed. Comparing MacCauley's drawing with photographs taken at the Pine Island village in the 1890s reveals that at the latter site, roof thatching extended down the sides nearly to the raised floor and also covered the ends of the buildings (fig. 4.5). Some of the Pine Island roofs have a hipped appearance, and the buildings in general appear to be

4.3. I-ful-lo-ha-tco's chickee as published in Clay MacCauley's 1887 Smithsonian report.

4.4. Inside view of chickee roof thatching, Big Cypress Reservation.

4.5. The Pine Island Seminole village about 1897, photographed by H. A. Ernst. (Reproduced with the permission of the Florida Anthropological Society and the Seminole Miccosukee Photographic Archives.)

more complex in style than the simple floor plan observed by MacCauley. Unfortunately, chickee-style architecture leaves little behind for the archaeologist to study, and relatively few archaeological sites containing chickee remains are known.

Because chickee architecture is versatile and relies solely on building materials available in the local environment, this style has persisted in use among contemporary Seminoles and has been adopted by non-Indian South Floridians for use in a variety of settings. Chickee bars abound, usually situated next to a pool at a hotel, resort, or marina, and I have seen them in backyards in Immokalee and elsewhere used to cover barbecues and patio furniture. Many of these are built by Seminoles as a commercial enterprise. Pickup trucks, their beds stacked high with cut palmetto fronds, can be seen hurtling through the vast "South Blocks" area of the defunct Golden Gates subdivision east of Naples (now the Picayune Strand State Forest) on their way to some building site, and piles of peeled cypress posts identify the homes of Seminole builders on the reservations.

The Cultural Landscape of the Big Cypress

The beginning date of Seminole settlement in the Big Cypress is not known with certainty. Sam Jones appears to have been one of the first, although his exact whereabouts remains elusive. During his long life, he was associated with locations ranging from coastal Hernando County north of Tampa to the Big Cypress, Sam Jones Island in the Pine Island complex, and ultimately a remote spot deep within the Everglades. Overall, however, archaeological sites attributable to Seminole occupation are rare in the Big Cypress prior to 1860. Military documents tell us that such sites did exist, so the problem is one of archaeological discovery and identification. Material culture during this era of war and conflict may have been greatly reduced and villages may not have been located in one place for very long, factors that may make them virtually invisible to the archaeologist.

The Seminole presence in the Big Cypress is increasingly detectable in the period between 1860 and 1900, and after the turn of the century scatters of broken glass jars, rusted metal enamel pans, fragments of aluminum and iron kettles, and machine-cut nails mark Seminole villages. The Seminoles made extensive use of the Big Cypress, but their presence was never intensive. Occasional piles of rock in some of the better-drained hammocks show attempts at farming, but more commonly oak trees were simply girdled and left to die, thereby opening up a clearing where orange trees,

4.6. Glass demijohn bottle, ca. 1850–1860, and French wine bottle, ca. 1860, from early Seminole camps located during the National Park Service survey of the Big Cypress region. (Photograph courtesy of the National Park Service, Southeastern Archaeological Center, Tallahassee.)

bananas, or papayas could be planted. Areas of girdled oaks are the most abundant indication of Seminole activities in the Big Cypress.

Village sites from any period are not numerous or large. One turn-of-the-century site discovered by National Park Service survey archaeologists in the southern Big Cypress (8MO1209) was a twenty meter by twenty meter occupation area with a surface scatter of glass bottle fragments, a sherd from a Hayner's Whiskey bottle dated to 1897, porcelain sherds, a blue faceted barrel bead, and pieces of rusted metal. Burned chickee posts marked a former structure, and a worn area nearby on the bank of the island indicated the canoe landing. In the eastern Big Cypress, a similarly dated site (8DA426) covered an area of about fifty meters by twenty meters and contained a cypress pier extending out into the slough. Here the archaeologists found another blue barrel bead, a medicine bottle, a Vaseline bottle, a stoneware jug, a green glass wine bottle dating back to about 1860 (fig. 4.6), and an iron shotgun.

Several well-known Seminoles lived in larger villages. Concho Billy's settlement dating to the 1930s consisted of a semicircular clearing with five chickees. Charlie Tiger Tail's village and trading post on Dixons Slough covered an area of about one hundred meters by twenty-five meters. Found here were a variety of round, barrel, and faceted beads, shell, plastic, and iron buttons, unfired .38-caliber bullets, a brass safe dial, and the iron safe from the store. A cane mill once stood at the site behind the store.

Burials were placed well away from living areas. Piles of stones or cypress posts from casket biers indicate areas where the Seminoles interred their dead. As they had for centuries, the Seminoles continued to send a person's possessions to the grave with him or her, and in so doing inadvertently created a bonanza for grave robbers and vandals driven by greed or a twisted sense of history to obtain objects for their own collections. Sadly, all archaeologically recorded Seminole graves in the Big Cypress have been vandalized. Strewn about on the surface of the grave sites are glass beads, plastic buttons, iron pots, bullets and gun parts, and in one case, an iron bullet mold and an oval-shaped bone cut from a human skull.

The ceremonial dance grounds, cleared areas in dry pine woods or hammocks, are the final pieces of the Seminole settlement pattern in the Big Cypress. In size, dance grounds cover more area than villages and can be as large as one hundred meters by three hundred meters. The dance grounds were used intensively for short periods of time, usually during the four days of the Green Corn Dance in early summer, but may have been returned to year after year. The next chapter will focus on the history of the Green Corn Dance and its importance in Seminole culture. But it is important to know that activities at the dance grounds left physical traces on the landscape and that the dance grounds are real geographical locations that should be treated with respect. In terms of archaeological preservation, dance ground sites can contain the remains of the clan chickees and objects dropped or discarded by the people staying there, such as bottle glass, broken plates, crockery, and eating utensils.

The cultural landscape of the Seminole occupation of the Big Cypress is that of a web in which village, garden, grave, and dance grounds were connected by foot paths or canoe trails.

Early Seminole Settlement in the Everglades

Contrary to popular belief, the true Everglades, that slowly flowing fifty-mile-wide river of grass centered on the Shark River Slough, is less central to Seminole history than the adjacent Big Cypress. Much of what is typically thought to be quintessentially Seminole as portrayed in postcard scenes and popular publications—the brightly colored patchwork vignettes set in the pole-and-thatch chickee camps—are in fact scenes of life in the Big Cypress. Today's Seminole and Miccosukee people for the most part do not live in the heart of the Everglades but instead occupy reservation lands in the center of the Big Cypress or at the eastern and western edges of the Glades.

Seminoles and Miccosukees did live on the tree islands in the Everglades, and the freshwater wetlands were important hunting and fishing grounds, but the true historical position of the Seminoles in the Everglades proper remains poorly known. Wide-ranging hunting in search of "pelts, plumes, and hides," in the words of historian Harry Kersey, certainly brought the Big Cypress and Okeechobee Seminoles into the Everglades, but did they live there, and if so, when and for how long?

These became important questions in the late 1930s when the federal government began taking steps to acquire territory for Everglades National Park, apparently, some claim, with little or no consideration for the native peoples already residing there. The focus of much of Seminole cultural history in the Everglades is on the eastern region along the Shark River corridor. To understand the historical importance of this area to contemporary Seminoles, we must first grapple with the problem of the so-called Spanish Indians.

The Question of the Spanish Indians

The notion that remnants of Florida's precontact native tribes survived into the nineteenth century continues to fascinate both the scholarly mind and popular imagination. Scattered but intriguing archaeological evidence mostly in the form of bull's-eye–stamped pottery sherds suggests the possibility that bands of Apalachee Indians moved south through Florida's gulf coast islands late in the seventeenth or early in the eighteenth centuries, eventually reaching Charlotte Harbor, the Ten Thousand Islands, and perhaps even the Florida Keys. Here, in the logic of this scenario, these refugees would have come in contact with small groups of surviving Calusa Indians, once dominant in the region, and, later, Spanish fishermen or individuals of mixed Spanish-Indian ancestry. Together, these groups came to share a common identity as "Spanish Indians" referred to in various documentary sources from the 1820s and 1830s. Alternate scenarios say the Calusa element was most important or that the Spanish Indians were a mix of Calusa and Seminole.

Adding to the confusion are various documentary morsels referring to the unique language of the Spanish Indians while failing to record any vocabulary. Most views on the origins of the Spanish Indians ultimately are brought to bear on this single question: Was the notorious Chakaika a Spanish Indian of Calusa ancestry, or was he a Seminole, descended from an early wave of Seminole immigrants into South Florida? Some of the best minds in Seminole ethnohistorical scholarship—William Sturtevant, Wilfred Neill, John Goggin, John Griffin—have focused attention on the case of Chakaika and the Spanish Indians. Still, the issue remains mysterious.

Although Chakaika's origins remain hidden from view, the events of his later life are known in some detail. In July 1839, the fourth year of the Second Seminole War, Chakaika joined forces with the Seminole Hospetarke to attack the camp and store established in the pine woods on the north bank of the Caloosahatchee River by Colonel William S. Harney. Harney himself was apparently the target of the attack but escaped in the river clad only in his underclothes, while thirteen of his thirty-two men (a total that included two civilian traders and two black interpreters) were killed immediately in the brief offensive. One trader lay dead under his hammock, the other, bleeding to death, had his skull crushed by the butt of a Seminole rifle. The two black interpreters made for the river but were captured. One of them, the unfortunate Sandy, was tortured to death four days later while tied to a tree, apparently on the orders of Sam Jones. The other, Sampson, lived as a captive for two years in the Big Cypress until his escape. Whatever the immediate tragic outcome of the attack on Harney, one thing was certain. Chakaika had entered the fray an unknown entity but paddled back to his Everglades stronghold loaded down with loot as a hated foe who had earned Harney's undying enmity.

Chakaika's next historical appearance took place just over one year later, on August 7, 1840, when seventeen canoes under his command beached on the small island of Indian Key in the northern Keys. Again, the attack centered on a store, this one part of a small village where the noted tropical botanist Henry Perrine lived with his family. Although his family escaped the attack, Dr. Perrine was trapped and killed in the cupola of his house. After putting much of the village to the torch, Chakaika and his band, several blacks among them, rowed four kegs of gunpowder, calico cloth, flour, tobacco, and other goods to Lower Matecumbe Key and from there carried them back to the Everglades.

Retaliation was delayed while the army gathered information on the exact whereabouts of Chakaika, Billy Bowlegs, the Prophet (Otulke-thloco), and Hospertacke, all known to be operating from Big Cypress and Everglades hideouts and feared by the army to be acting together from a unified plan. All but Chakaika were ostensibly listening to offers of peace brought by "friendly" Creeks from Arkansas ("friendly" meaning sympathetic to the U.S. goals of Indian removal) but were more or less biding their time.

In December 1840, Harney and his dragoons, assisted by the Third Artillery, threaded their way through the mud, marsh, and water of the Everglades, intent on returning with no less than Chakaika's scalp. Isolated chickee camps and corn fields encountered by the troops told them that they were on the right track. Finally, the soldiers slogged out of the swamp and burst in on Chakaika's camp in a dawn raid on December 10, 1840. The surprised Chakaika was shot through the brain and fell dead face down in the water. His scalped body was strung up from one of the large trees on the island. The plunder from the Indian Key and previous raids was auctioned off to the soldiers on the spot. Returning to Key Biscayne by means of the Shark River, Harney found more chickee villages and indicated his interest in mounting a second expedition targeting the island of Sam Jones. This he attempted the following month, entering the eastern Everglades through the New River, only to find that the wily Sam Jones had removed to the Big Cypress.

Historians and anthropologists likely will squabble without end about Chakaika's cultural identity, but for the Seminoles the issue is more certain. He was one of them, they claimed in interviews recorded by William Sturtevant in the early 1950s. Seminole oral traditions told of hostile encounters with previous inhabitants of South Florida, presumably telling of some real encounters between early Creeks or Seminoles and Calusa people, but Chakaika, they say, was not of the latter group. Rather, Chakaika was a leader of an eastern band of Mikasuki-speaking Seminoles who entered the Everglades as his western counterparts were entering the Big Cypress. This scenario, of course, places a Seminole group firmly in the Everglades at a relatively early date, perhaps before the outbreak of the Second Seminole War, and thus bolsters the case of the contemporary Miccosukee along the Tamiami Trail that the Everglades is ancestral land.

The logic of this scenario would suggest that not only Chakaika but the Spanish Indians as well were actually Seminoles whose descendants are numbered among the modern Miccosukee Tribe. However, this story seems to remove the "Spanish" from the Spanish-Indian nomenclature. This version also is difficult to reconcile with accounts from around the turn of the century that speak of encounters in the southern Everglades with Indians who were not in custom and appearance "Seminole." It is perhaps easier to think of this group as descended from the survivors of

Chakaika's band, all of them a cultural fusion of Calusa, Spaniard, and Seminole traits.

Despite the many uncertainties of history and the cultural mysteries that likely will remain unresolved, one thing is certain. The emotional association between the Everglades and Seminole cultural identity is very strong. No matter what history tells us, today the Seminoles seem to be an integral part of the story of this vast watery realm, and it a part of them.

The Pine Island Ridge and Seminole Settlement
in the Eastern Everglades

During the first several decades of the 1800s the Seminoles found their way across or around the Everglades to the high sandy ground of the Pine Island group of islands. In the geological past, before there was an Everglades, these islands were dunes keeping the sea from South Florida, but the Seminoles were not much concerned with this. To them, the islands were oases of dry land where crops could be grown, coontie could be gathered, and plenty of space was available for the dance ceremonies. To the Seminoles, the Pine Islands were a refuge when the U.S. military began their search-and-destroy missions in the Big Cypress during the Second Seminole War.

Ultimately the islands proved to be no safe haven when Colonel Harney directed his efforts at the relentless pursuit of Sam Jones in 1840. Shortly thereafter the islands appear prominently on military maps of the area, and Pine Island, Chittos Island, Mud Island, Council Island, Prophets Island, and Sam Jones Island enter the documentary record (fig. 4.7). These maps also make clear the crux of Harney's concern: the Pine Islands were a natural conduit for movement back and forth to the Shark River Slough, stronghold of the hated Chakaika and a deep pocket of the Seminole resistance. Until the islands were controlled, future buildup of Seminole strength in the Shark River area would always be a potential threat.

The Seminoles had invested considerable labor in clearing the islands according to their needs, and their villages had an air of permanence. A member of Harney's force described Chittos Island as having two towns, each with its own dance ground, and a shared council lodge. With the exception of the dance grounds and a small garden of Cuban tobacco, the island was covered with pumpkin, squash, and melon vines, and "luxuriant" growth of lima beans. The Seminoles had fled the island some weeks before and had left behind, in the words of the soldier, "useless" items such as war dance masks, baskets, kettles, bows, and fishing spears. These ob-

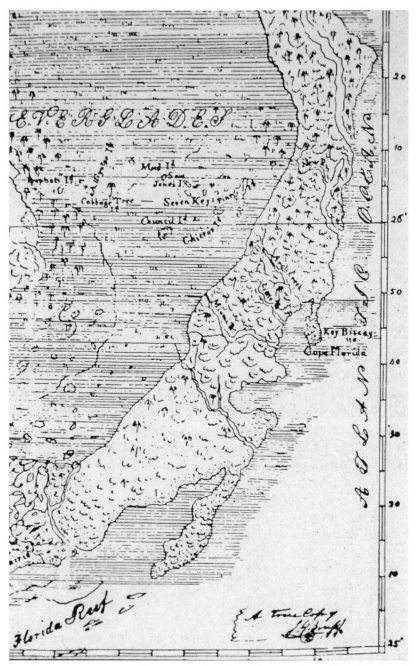

4.7. An 1841 military map from the National Archives showing Pine Island and other Seminole locations in the eastern Everglades.

4.8. Brass arrow point from Snake Warriors Island. (Photograph courtesy of the Archaeological and Historical Conservancy.)

jects suggest a culture not in decline but rather one fully adapted to its ecological setting and with its political and religious realms alive and well.

Although these wonderful items of Seminole material culture did not survive, Chittos Island itself experienced a more positive fate. Slated for development as a subdivision and shopping center, the core area of the island was saved from the bulldozer and preserved through state acquisition in 1992 by the quick action and coordinated efforts of the Trust for Public Lands and the Archaeological and Historical Conservancy, located in Miami. Last-ditch archaeology done by the Conservancy provided sufficient evidence that the real estate was in fact Chittos Island, or Snake Warriors Island in translation. Glass beads, a metal arrow point (fig. 4.8), wrought iron spikes, musket balls, and a U.S. Army hat buckle, individually not overly dramatic finds, together told enough of the story to make a compelling case for preservation. Having satisfied the criteria of Florida's Emergency Archaeological Acquisition Act of 1988, Snake Warriors Island became public property with the approval of the governor and cabinet. It is now managed by the Broward County Department of Parks and Recreation.

A similar sequence of events resulted in preservation by state acquisition of a portion of Pine Island Ridge. The adjacent Ranch Ridge parcel, apparently once containing a large Seminole village and dance ground, was subsequently purchased by the town of Davie and is now similarly protected from development. Snake Warriors Island and the Pine Island Ridge saw a resurgence of Seminole settlement after the Seminole wars, but it was Pine Island that was ultimately to become the major hub of Seminole life and ceremonial activity in southeastern Florida. At least three major clan camps existed there by the end of the nineteenth century, and the Green Corn, or busk, Dance, the Hunting Dance, and the Snake Dance were held there with regularity. Travel between the islands was by foot when the

4.9. Present-day view of the portion of the Pine Island Ridge once occupied by the Seminoles, preserved as green space by the town of Davie.

season was dry and in times of high water, in sailing canoes hewn from huge cypress logs.

Life was good for the Pine Island Seminoles, at least for a time. Visitors to the villages in the 1880s remarked on the comfort of the chickee camps, the pleasant natural surroundings, and the bright and active Seminole children hunting small game with their bows and arrows. When Snake Warriors Island began to be swallowed up by encroaching development, its people moved to the Pine Island complex, making this even more of a nuclear area. In its prime, the Pine Island complex, including Long Key and Big City Island, was home to as many as two hundred Seminoles. Pumpkins and lima beans grew in abundance. Potatoes, bananas, and corn also did well in the hammock soil. Coontie roots were grubbed from nearby woods. Bird plumes, hides, and furs went to the Stranahan store in Fort Lauderdale or the Brickell store on the Miami River in exchange for pots and pans, powder and bullets, glass beads and cloth.

By the early years of the twentieth century, the days of the Pine Island refuge were numbered. Government agents such as A. J. Duncan and the surveyor J. O. Fries recognized that the Seminoles belonged on the Pine Islands but ultimately were unable to preserve the lands for them. The further expansion of white settlement and drainage of the eastern Everglades by newly constructed canals spelled the demise of the Seminole way of life, and by the end of the twentieth century's first decade, the dispersal of the Pine Island groups was complete. Historian Patsy West estimates that 40 percent of today's Seminoles are descended from the Pine Island bands, including members of the Seminole Tribe on the Hollywood, Big Cypress, and Brighton reservations and members of the Miccosukee Tribe residing on the Tamiami Trail. In recent years, keen-eyed archaeologists have spotted only fragments of bottle glass and the occasional colored glass bead erupting from the sands of the ridge (fig. 4.9), weak testimony of the dancing, ball play, and vibrant village life that once took place here.

Okeechobee Groups—Catfish Creek

While Sam Jones, Billy Bowlegs, and the southern bands moved between the Big Cypress and the eastern Everglades, other events were taking place in the pine flatwoods and hill-and-lake country above Lake Okeechobee. Involved were people ancestral to today's Brighton Seminoles. These were the Muskogee-speaking Seminoles, with cultural roots among the Upper Creeks of central Alabama. When these groups arrived in Florida is still an open question, but it is possible that they are the "Tallasays" of the Second Seminole War documents. It is also possible that the Muskogee speakers kept the native pottery-making tradition alive and that the brushed pottery vessels reported by archaeologists from the Kissimmee valley south of Orlando mark the southern movement of the Tallasays from uplands in north and west-central Florida (fig. 4.10).

The man most often talked about in the historical record of Seminole activity in this area is known as Chipco. Some have said that he was born in Alabama between 1800 and 1805. By 1818, Chipco was living in the major Seminole village at Old Town on the Suwannee River when it was attacked by Andrew Jackson. Historian Albert De Vane indicates that Chipco settled in the upper Peace River vicinity and then on Lake Thonotosassa near the

4.10. Seminole pottery vessels from Central Florida, probably dating to the late eighteenth or early nineteenth century.

Hillsborough River east of Tampa in the 1820s, movements that reflect the diaspora of Seminoles from the Suwannee and Alachua areas following the Jackson offensive and the attacks of the Georgians. Chipco claimed to have participated in the attack on Dade's command on December 28, 1835, which if true, would place him in the general vicinity of the Cove of the Withlacoochee in the early war years. Unfortunately, Sprague's standard reference on the Second Seminole War fails to make any mention of Chipco.

Local oral histories suggest that Chipco, Tallahassee, Billy Bowlegs, Billy Buster, Johnny Jumper, and Robert Osceola settled on an island in Lake Hamilton south of Haines City during the war to evade capture and involvement in the hostilities. This memory may relate to the Third Seminole War period, 1855–1858, rather than the era of the Second Seminole War, but nonetheless it appears that Lake Hamilton was one stop of many for this group through the late decades of the 1800s. When the Lake Hamilton village was visited by the landowner in 1890, long after its abandonment by the Seminoles, he found a large live oak log hollowed out as a mortar for pounding corn and a large hewn cypress canoe. The story of the Lake Hamilton settlement is told by a historical marker on U.S. Highway 27 just south of the lake.

Whatever the specific sequence of events, military efforts to precisely locate the band in 1857–1858 in the area between Catfish Lake and Lake Marian failed. One soldier left flags for the Seminoles pointing the direction to the army camp. When they returned, the flags had been moved to face the trackless swamp, presumably in the direction of the Indian camps. After a three-day trek, the army lost this game of "come and get me."

Chipco moved east to the Kissimmee valley for a time in the late 1860s and returned to the hilly lake region by 1872, settling at Catfish Lake, known today as Lake Pierce and within view of the famous Bok Tower. Here he was visited by Captain R. H. Pratt in 1879 and Clay MacCauley during his reconnaissance of 1880. They found that two camps had been established on the uplands fringing the south side of the lake. Chipco remarked to Pratt that the needs of his band were few and declined any assistance from Washington. MacCauley, however, observed that Chipco's fields and the surrounding forest failed to provide him with the bounty noted at the Big Cypress and Everglades villages. In fact, their sweet potato harvest had been decimated by marauding animals, forcing a trip further north to the coontie grounds on Horse Creek near Fort Davenport. Here they built temporary shedlike lodges covered with palmetto leaves, unlike the cotton tents used by the southern bands on their foraging trips.

Other cultural oddities of Chipco's Seminoles were commented on by MacCauley, whom they took to calling "Doctor Na-ki-ta" or "Doctor what is it" because of his persistent questioning. Catfish Lake men tended to wear kerchiefs tied around their heads more than did the Everglades and Big Cypress Seminoles and in general paid less attention to their personal appearance, said MacCauley. But MacCauley was particularly taken with the so-called progressive behavior of Me-le, son of a Seminole Indian father and a black mother, who built a frame house, quite unlike the prevailing chickee-style residence, and was cultivating a grove of oranges. Mac-Cauley's interpreter, Billy Ko-nip-ha-tco, also was an outcast because of his nontraditional attitudes, to the point of being threatened with death by his Big Cypress relatives, so MacCauley's sympathies may have favored this attitude. Although Me-le had been adopted into the band as a child, he was shunned by his cohorts as an adult.

Chipco had no such problem and was renowned for his good nature and ability to get along with his white neighbors (despite the implication of his earlier involvement in the murder of the white youth). He was often seen among them in Haines City and Tampa and was reputed to be wealthy, at least by the standards of that time and place. Supposed firsthand observations of Chipco and his gold coins prompted treasure hunting even then in search of buried loot. What happened to Chipco's possessions upon his death in 1881 is not known with certainty beyond reports that his gun, hunting equipment, cooking utensils, favorite horse, dog, and several other horses were killed to accompany him on the journey to the next world.

Chipco's nephew Tallahassee assumed leadership of the band just before Chipco's death and lived first at a Catfish Lake camp before moving to a new location on Lake Rosalie. Here Tallahassee continued the tradition of friendship with the local white settlers and is said to have saved entire families from starvation with timely gifts of turkey and deer. By the early years of the 1880s, however, the Catfish Lake camps had been abandoned and had moved south to the vicinity of Cow Creek, a small tributary feeding into Lake Okeechobee's north shore. There they were joined by camps from Fish Eating Creek, together forming the Cow Creek band from which today's Brighton Seminoles are descended.

→ 5 ←

Of Busks and Bundles

↑　↑　↑　↑　↑　↑　↑　↑　↑　↑　↑　↑　↑

In the aboriginal Southeast no greater human drama was played out than when the people gathered for the rites of purification, known in historic times as the busk or Green Corn Dance. Archaeologists think that the concern for ritual purity has deep roots in southeastern prehistory, going back at least 2,000 years to the beginning of the mound-building cultures. Large conch shell dippers or cups found buried in these early mounds indicate the existence of the black drink ceremony, say the archaeologists, a ceremony known to have been practiced by the Timucuans and other early historic-period Indians and later an integral part of the Creek and Seminole Green Corn Dance.

Archaeological evidence also indicates that the peoples of late prehistory, peoples of the Mississippian archaeological culture, brought the purification rituals to their climax, even elevating them to the status of an organized or institutionalized religion. Both the ceremonial mounds constructed by the Mississippians and the ritual objects they made tell us something of their beliefs and practices. An observer sitting on the outskirts of any of the large southeastern mound centers may have watched as a masked and feathered dancer threaded his way through plumes of smoke around a dance fire atop a large ceremonial mound, the villagers and people from outlying hamlets watching from below. Such scenes were played out among cultures as far east as the St. Johns River of Florida all the way west to the Mississippi River.

Historical accounts of aboriginal religious practices dating to the early years of the European presence in the Southeast are few. Most of the transplanted Europeans had more pressing concerns, such as subduing other Europeans or the Indians who stood in their way. One famous account of the black drink ceremony among the Timucuans of North Florida comes from the narrative of Jacques Le Moyne, artist and cartographer of the ill-fated Ribaut colony at Fort Caroline in the early 1560s. According to Le Moyne, council meetings opened with the chief drinking boiled *cassina* (the ilex or holly leaves used to make the black drink) from a shell cup, which was then passed to brave warriors seated to his left and right. Le Moyne's narrative states that the object was to keep the drink down (thus proving your bravery and worth), but the accompanying woodcut shows that vomiting was a frequent result.

First Glimpses of the Green Corn Dance

In the eighteenth century, when the Europeans had established themselves among the southeastern Indians and had gained their favor by conducting trade among them, observations of Indian religion become more numerous and complete. Here we see the busk, from the Creek *poskita*, meaning "to fast," in all its richness and complexity. The Irish trader James Adair witnessed busks among the southeastern Indians in the 1760s. Although his narrative was heavily flavored with biblical comparisons, it captured the essential elements of the ceremony that were to persist for the next one hundred and fifty years.

According to Adair, the festival started with a two-day fast, after which great energy was spent cleaning and refurbishing the square and the grounds where the ceremony was to take place, to clean it of "every supposed polluting thing." Central to this was the removal and disposal of the old hearth. Tobacco, button snakeroot, and other herbs were placed in the hearth and then covered over with a fresh layer of white clay. Above the new hearth warriors constructed an arbor of green branches. Warrior guards kept intruders from the purified ground; meanwhile at home the women cleaned out their domestic hearths and cleansed their pottery vessels. The warriors maintained the fast by drinking a tea made from the bitter snakeroot, causing them to vomit and bringing about a higher state of purity.

At the close of the third day all prepared for the new fire ceremony. Home fires were extinguished at the direction of the priest. Fire, newly kindled by a fire drill, was first taken to the new hearth. Food, button snakeroot, and cassina were offered up by the priest for consecration. Then he addressed the men and women separately, berating, admonishing, and encouraging them to live their lives according to virtue and purity. All who had acted improperly during the previous year were forgiven as the light of the new fire shone upon them. Sticks burning with the new fire were then placed at the edge of the squareground so that each family could take a portion home for their own new fire. While this was being done, the priest supervised the parching of cassina leaves on the new fire and their boiling in a special pot to make the black drink. This bitter drink was then consumed by him and other elders for the duration of the ceremony.

On the fourth day the men and women gathered for feasting and dancing. The dancing was done in circles around the sacred fire to the music of clay-pot drums and gourd rattles. The men engaged in a mock battle, then the grand finale was called for. The women, wearing their finest silver earrings, strings of beads, silver wrist bands, with turtle shell rattles tied to their legs, joined the men in the dance circle. The ceremony culminated with the priest leading men, women, and children in a ritual cleansing bath in a nearby stream.

Adair describes a second ceremony, held in the spring and presumably before the new fire or busk "fast" ceremony. This four-day ceremony began with three days of dancing. The men wore painted gourd masks, and some wore buffalo horns and tails. Between dances, the men went hunting to bring in venison, which the women then dressed, cooked, and provided for all to share. After eating, the Indians fixed a large pole in the ground with a bush tied at the top. Over this bush a ball was thrown in the ball play, with men against women. They met every day for this game until the new corn was ready to be eaten.

John Howard Payne, observing perhaps the last of the Creek Green Corn Dances before their removal to the West, described a scene of great intensity and emotion. He had traveled to the squareground in the wilderness outside the town of Tukabahchee in central Alabama, a place where whites were tolerated if they kept to themselves and did not offend ritual protocol.

Four solid, open-fronted cabins formed a central square. Just beyond the square and off to one side was the council house, a conical-shaped building with a small ramped entrance cut into the earth. The council house sat at the corner of a second, smaller square, two sides of which were formed by cornfields, one by a low embankment, and one by the back of the buildings forming the main square. In the center of the council house square was a tall mound made from layers of earth scraped from the surface of the squareground every year before the ceremony. A second smaller mound, made of ashes from the sacred fires of previous years, stood just beyond one of the openings of the main square. This is where Payne stood to watch.

Payne arrived on the third day of the eight-day ceremony, too late to see the lighting of the sacred fire but in time to see huge pots of the black drink boiling on it. With great solemnity, the men lined up in the square to wait their turn for a gourdful of the drink. Afterward, each man with no apparent discomfort vomited what had just been imbibed. The chief then gave a speech and the dancing began. In one, each dancer held a feathered cane and danced in commemoration of victories at the ball game. In other dances, according to Payne's information, success at hunting bears, panthers, and buffalos was marked. The third day concluded with the ritual bloodletting of boys and young men, a test of will and endurance. Using sail-needles, awls, and flints, the elders cut into the outstretched arms of the youths, who were to take the pain without wincing.

The fourth day began with the ritual display of the famed "Tukabahchee plates," circular shields of brass and steel, in Payne's words. No one knows for sure where, how, or when the Indians got these plates, and the Indians themselves did not know. Some anthropologists think they were a gift from the Shawnee who had once lived among them, but no known tradition preserves this event. But what riveted Payne's attention on this fourth day was the Gun Dance, an elaborate frenzy of orchestrated chaos involving the ritual capture and scalping of four stuffed dummies placed at the corners of the smaller square. After the Gun Dance, the first ears of new corn were eaten. On the fifth day the men took to the forests to hunt deer. The next day, after watching the women dance in the central square (a spectacle Payne had missed on Day 2), Payne left and thus did not see the second fast day (Day 7) and the closing oration by the chief on Day 8.

Through time and across space the busk or Green Corn ritual clearly was as complex and diverse as the Southeastern Indians themselves. It embodied not only the beliefs and practices of the prehistoric mound builders but also the unique histories and cultural circumstances of each tribe. Not all elements were present in every ceremony, and not all were given the same importance from tribe to tribe. Some lasted four days, others eight. According to anthropologist John Swanton, the first four days of an eight-day ceremony were concerned with the purification of vegetable foods, the final four with animal foods. But what of those ceremonies with only four days? The Tukabahchee ceremony witnessed by Payne lacked the ball game so integral elsewhere and may have lacked the formal "court day" during which time all transgressions (except murder) were forgiven. The Gun Dance he described seems almost to have been the climax of the ceremony, a time when men and women participated together, a role more usually fulfilled by the ball game. The form that any particular Green Corn ceremony took reflected the specifics of time, place, and tradition. Yet at the core was a unity of ritual concerns.

To purify one's community before the spirit world by lighting the new fire, to purify one's flesh by fasting and scarification, and to achieve balance with the social, natural, and spiritual realms of existence by dancing and atonement, these were at the center of the Southeastern Indian busk.

The Florida Seminole Green Corn Dance is a distilled version of the annual busk ceremony of the southeastern Indians and has carried forward into the present day its core ritual elements. Sadly, we know little about the history of the Green Corn Dance among the Seminoles. William Bartram, so eloquent in his passages concerning eighteenth-century Seminole culture, was not privy to information about the great ceremony. Other narratives of Seminole life during this time are likewise mute concerning the dance. The British colonial authorities in St. Augustine knew that the practice existed, but they knew nothing of the particulars or its cultural significance. It was probably the case that the Indians kept such knowledge from them, although as we have seen, the more secular or political calumet ceremony was brought into the British domain. The Spanish in Florida perhaps cared even less what Indians were doing, particularly after the ultimate failure of the mission system, and there is no indication that the Seminoles felt inclined to tell them.

During the Second Seminole War (1835–1842), the Americans likewise knew of but never witnessed the Seminole Green Corn Dance. Dance grounds were occasionally discovered by advancing troops, and areas in the Withlacoochee swamps near Lake Panasoffkee and in the Big Cypress were known to be favored ceremonial locations. But unlike the Tukabahchee Creeks with whom John Howard Payne visited, the Seminoles did not open their ceremony to tourists, particularly in the midst of war.

It was not until 1880 that we get a written description of the Seminole Green Corn Dance (not actually published until 1884), and this was little more than a sketch by Clay MacCauley based on reluctant informant information. MacCauley visited the Florida Seminoles in the winter of 1880–1881, not the right time of the year to observe the busk, but he probably would have been kept from it had he showed up in June. He tells us that on the first day of the four-day ceremony, the black drink is taken and the Medicine Song sung. On the morning of the second day, ears of green corn are eaten. The third day is one of fasting, while the fourth and final day sees great feasting or "Hom-pi-ta-clak-o."

Clearly MacCauley was given only the most superficial information about the ceremony. The drawing he provides with his text (fig. 5.1) must have been reconstructed by him based on what he was told and not from firsthand observation. Here we see the clear and persistent importance of the central fire, but a new element, the medicine fire, has been added. Evi-

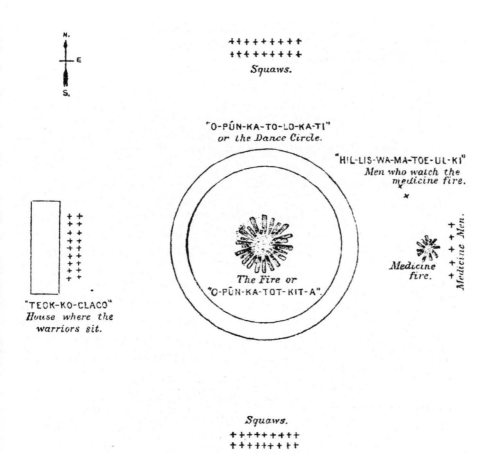

5.1. Seminole Green Corn Dance grounds as published in Clay MacCauley's 1887 Smithsonian report. The drawing was probably done on the basis of composite oral testimony rather than firsthand observation.

dently the medicine men from each group had a seat by the medicine fire, while others, the "men who watch the medicine fire" sat nearby. This aspect of the Seminole ceremony bears no great similarity to that of the Creeks described by Payne in 1835, and with MacCauley's account, no matter how unsatisfactory, we begin to understand that there has been a significant transformation in the Green Corn Dance as practiced by the Seminoles. A concern for the "medicine" has grown strong, and the medicine men now issue the call summoning the people to the dance grounds (in the same way the Creeks did it, by passing out like-numbered bundles of sticks) and preside over its ritual. Their main area of responsibility involved the care and display of the medicine bundle, something not known to us from earlier descriptions of the Creek ceremony.

The Medicine

When the association between medicine bundles and the busk ceremony first developed among the Florida Seminoles is not known with precision. As we will see, anthropologists in the twentieth century took great care to describe the central importance of the bundles to the Seminole Green Corn Dance of that era. Some have surmised that the emergence of medicine bundles as sacred objects correlates with the downscaling of society that occurred during the Second Seminole War and the increased need for war magic during this period. In this view, the bundle, the keeper of the bundle or the medicine man, and the dance grounds became the spiritual core of Seminole life during or just after the war and became the main focal point for social and political organization in the years of isolation. Above the domestic level of the clan camp, people were pulled together as members of busk groups for the annual Green Corn ceremony, each group having its own medicine bundle (or bundles) and medicine man knowledgeable of its contents. Green Corn ceremonies were no longer gatherings of the town and its outlying farmsteads, as was the case in Creek country, but were gatherings of distant, even isolated, family camps into a busk group. Where chiefs once had wielded their authority around the great fire of the central square, now medicine men carefully unwrapped the contents of their deerskin bundles. By the 1950s three busk groups existed, one centered north of Lake Okeechobee composed of Muskogee speakers, and the other two, with five bundles between them, composed of Mikasuki speakers in the Everglades–Big Cypress area.

What was in the medicine bundles? They contained objects so powerful, it was said, that mishandling by the medicine man could bring sickness and harm to the busk group. The bundle could turn its power on its own busk group in this case, "eating their blood" and causing pains in the head and joints. They contained objects whose care and safekeeping were considered vital to the health of the group and objects at first whose properties kept the Seminoles from harm in time of war, the "Power of War" medicines. One such medicine was the Thunder Missile, a small crystal that either drove the soldiers into an agitated state or made the Indian warriors invisible to them. Another medicine made of silvery powder, possibly of plant origin, could put soldiers to sleep. Another small stone in the bundle could be magically enlarged to act as a shield to deflect bullets. Fangs from a rattlesnake were used to scratch the arms and legs of warriors, giving them extra strength and making them unafraid. Ginseng imported from North Florida or Oklahoma and wrapped in white cloth inside the bundle served as "shot-in-the-heart" medicine for warriors wounded in battle.

Warfare alone was not the only domain of the medicine bundles. Hunting magic was also well represented among medicine bundle objects. One of these was the "Snake Horn," a small white sphere obtained by a hunter from the underwater horned snake, which could help the hunter attract deer. Bones of the "Little People," small humanlike beings who lived in trees, also acted as hunting charms. The special flint used to start the medicine fire at the Green Corn ceremony was also kept in the bundle, wrapped in a cow horn or in its own wooden container. A single medicine bundle, itself nearly an entire deerskin complete with the head and leg skin, could contain hundreds of objects individually wrapped in skin or cloth. Each was unwrapped and displayed to the busk group by the medicine man. Some were too powerful to touch and had to be handled with a tweezerlike pair of buzzard wing bones.

Where did the medicine bundles come from? How did they come to the Seminoles? The Seminoles say that the first medicine was given to the original medicine men, one of the Wind clan, one of the Tiger clan, by the Old Man. The medicine men were told how to use the medicine by a voice singing a song, one song for each medicine. Oral histories are difficult to unravel on this point and vary according to the language and specific cultural tradition of the speaker. In one version an owl and a rattlesnake agree to give claws and fangs to a monkeylike character who holds on to the medicines until a human figure comes on the scene. In another, the delivery of the medicines is connected to the arrival of the son of the Corn Mother, who also promotes the use of corn. Regardless, the knowledge of the medicines was so vast and complex that two medicine men were needed to understand it all. All the medicines were together in one bundle until the Second Seminole War, when they were divided into smaller bundles carried by individual war parties. Some of these bundles were carried west with the Seminoles deported to Indian Territory, but a number survived in Florida.

By the time Clay MacCauley visited (but unknown to him) nine bundles existed. Two of these were accidentally burned in a fire in 1895; a third burned in 1908. One of the six remaining bundles was cared for by a medicine man of the Muskogee-speaking Cow Creek band and is the core of that busk group. The other five were Mikasuki and eventually were divided among busk groups centered in the Big Cypress and along the Tamiami Trail. Although in strict historical terms the origin of the medicine bundles, or the first bundle, is not known, a direct historical connection to the Second Seminole War does exist. The bundles form a direct physical and spiritual link between the Seminoles of the present and their ancestors who fought the likes of Taylor, Jesup, Scott, and Gaines. In no other southeastern Indian society do medicine bundles play a similar role. Closest perhaps were the Tukabahchee plates of the Creeks, but these seem to have been limited to that town only and lacked the complex meanings associated with the Seminole bundles. The cultural identity of the Seminoles and the existence of the medicine bundles are bound together inseparably. Once we understand this, the central importance of the medicine bundles to the Seminoles can be appreciated.

By the turn of the twentieth century only a few white men were rumored to have seen the Seminole busk, and none to our knowledge wrote about it. Anthropologists knew the busk ceremony was alive among the Seminoles. Alexander Spoehr made notes on it in the 1930s from information given him by the Cow Creeks. On May 28, 1943, John Goggin saw twenty-five Indian cars parked along the Tamiami Trail two miles east of Turners River and knew that it meant that the Green Corn Dance was under way in a hammock nearby. But the first recorded eyewitness accounts do not come until the 1950s. Louis Capron attended the Cow Creek dance and questioned some of his Mikasuki-speaking friends about the ceremony as practiced in that group. William Sturtevant followed up on Capron's observations several years later, checking further details with his Mikasuki informants, describing the medicines in some detail, and commenting on the differences and similarities between the Cow Creek and Mikasuki ceremonies.

From them we learn that the Seminole busk typically lasted four days. The dates varied according to group, and the ceremony could occur from late April through mid-July. Specific dates were chosen each year by the medicine man and his assistant and reflect a period of time about four months after the planting of the new corn. When the time was right, members of the various clans of the busk group arrived at the dance grounds and constructed temporary camps for themselves nearby (fig. 5.2). At the center of the dance ground was the fire, around it, the circular dance track. Just beyond the dance circle to the northeast or southeast was the ball pole, a pine or cypress tree with its branches removed. On the west side of the dance circle was a rectangular arbor, open facing east. Opposite to the east

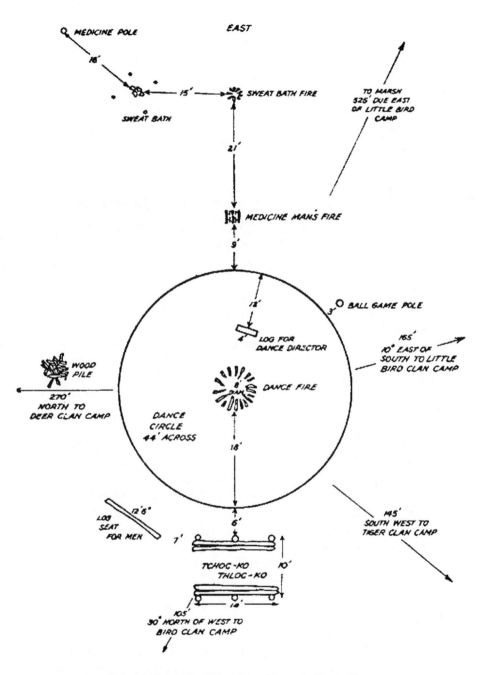

EAST

MEDICINE POLE

18′

SWEAT BATH FIRE

15′

TO MARSH
525′ DUE EAST
OF LITTLE BIRD
CAMP

SWEAT BATH

21′

MEDICINE MAN'S FIRE

9′

BALL GAME POLE

3′

18′

155′
10° EAST OF
SOUTH TO LITTLE
BIRD CLAN CAMP

LOG FOR
DANCE DIRECTOR

4′

WOOD
PILE

270°
NORTH TO
DEER CLAN CAMP

8′ DIAM   DANCE FIRE

DANCE
CIRCLE
44′ ACROSS

18′

145′
SOUTH WEST TO
TIGER CLAN CAMP

12′ 6″

LOG
SEAT
FOR MEN

7′

6′

TCHOC-KO
THLOC-KO

10′

14′

105′
30° NORTH OF WEST TO
BIRD CLAN CAMP

5.2. Ground plan of the Green Corn Dance by Louis Capron.

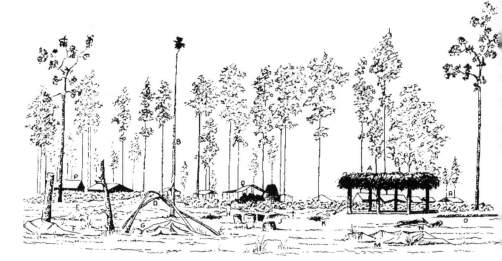

5.3. Louis Capron's sketch of the Green Corn dance grounds, 1949, based on a photograph. *A*, the Tchoc-ko thloc-ko or "Big House," where men of all the clans met and where Court Day was held; *B*, the ball game pole; *C*, the stake for the medicine bundle; *D*, the sweat bath frame; *E*, the smoke of the sweat bath fire; *F*, a covering tarp; *G*, the sweat bath tarp; *H*, the smoke of the medicine man's fire; *I*, the dance circle; *J*, log seat of the dance director; *K*, the dance fire; *L*, pails of the black drink; *M*, a tarp; *N*, a log pile; *O*, a log seat for men; *P*, Little Bird clan camp; *Q*, Tiger clan camp; *R*, Bird clan camp.

was the medicine fire (much as MacCauley showed), the sweat bath, and the stake for hanging the medicine bundle (fig. 5.3).

The first day of the ceremony was spent gathering wood for the fires, cleaning the grounds, and preparing for what was to come. The medicine man began the day with a ceremonial bath. In the afternoon, young men and women played a vigorous game of ball around the pole. At dusk, the dance fire was lit and various dances began.

The second day, Picnic Day, focused on eating foods brought to the grounds by the women. Men ate in the arbor (or Big House) while women ate in their camps. The afternoon and evening again were times of the ball play and dancing.

On the third day the ceremony was building toward a climax. The events of this day, Court Day or Fasting Day, occurred under the strict guidance of the medicine man. Three black drinks were prepared using button snake-root, willow, ginseng, and the leaves of various other plants. The medicine bundle was brought from its hiding place and then hung on the pole on the east side of the dance circle. The Feather Dance took place (but not every year), and the first of the black drinks were consumed by the men. As had always been the case in the aboriginal Southeast, the black drink caused vomiting. In addition, no food was to be eaten.

At noon the men gathered in the Big House for the annual council. Any man guilty of a transgression against Seminole society since the previous busk ceremony could now atone for his actions before his elders, usually the medicine man, men from other clans, advisors from other groups, and special busk officials from the Tiger, Wind, and Bird clans. In the best case, the crime was "killed," forgotten about once and for all, and the transgressor was made one again with society. At nightfall, the medicine fire was lit using the flint kept for that purpose in the medicine bundle. The bundle was opened, its contents examined and laid out. An ear of green corn was placed at each compass point of the medicine fire and the third black drink was boiled. At midnight, the four ears of roasted green corn were added to the pot, and the Big Gathered Medicine was ready. Four drinks were taken by each man, again followed by vomiting. The net result was to make the eating of the new corn safe for the rest of the year. But the men had to stay on their fast and not fall asleep.

The Green Corn Dance itself was danced at midnight. Around the central fire, other dances continued all night. By the medicine fire, adolescent boys ready to receive their adult names gathered and waited. When the time was right their new names were summoned forth from the afterworld by the men and proclaimed in the presence of the medicine man.

At dawn the medicine man looked at the individual medicines in the bundle, rewrapped them, and moved off into the woods to hide it. In the camps, women were preparing food for the men to break their fast. All men who had not previously done so submitted to scratching, ritual bloodletting through the use of sewing needles mounted to a wooden or quill frame. Not a punishment, this scratching was done to promote good health by letting out bad blood. Scratching was followed up by a sweat bath in the small structure built for that purpose. When the medicine man returned from the woods, the fast was broken by eating the green corn and other foods brought in by the women. Women had been able to eat the green corn all along, but the men had not, because they would become violently ill, it was believed, if they ate it before the busk ceremony. By the afternoon of the fourth day, camps were broken up and people began heading home.

As many as a dozen different dances were danced during the annual busk from a total repertoire of more than forty, each of them precisely choreographed and accompanied by music made by rattles (fig. 5.4) or, in the

5.4. Turtle shell leg rattles used in Seminole dances.

Buffalo Dance, a drum. Most dances were named in honor of specific animals, with the dance steps and motions meant to imitate that animal's movements. All dances except the Feather Dance were open to both men and women and thus were one major way in which men's and women's activities were brought together during the busk. The other major occasion for male-female interaction was the ball game. Because of its clear importance to the Seminoles and because the ball game is one important way in which Seminole culture is linked to the aboriginal Southeast, we must now take a closer look at its origins and history.

Seminole Ball Game

Two distinct types of ball game were played in the aboriginal Southeast. One of these, played on a field with goals at either end, appears to have been largely recreational, at least in the historic period when observed among the Seminoles, Choctaws, Creeks, and others. This was the famed "little brother of war," played between towns who were linked together for that purpose. Early travelers among the Seminoles, William Bartram for one, knew the Seminoles were playing this game and talked about its sometimes violent consequences. Micanopy's town at Okahumpka was a favorite site of this type of ball game in the early 1800s, and Micanopy's own ball stick was allegedly taken in a military raid on the nearby Black Seminole village of Pelaklikaha in 1836.

The other ball game, the single-pole game, existed it seems in the realm of ritual. Not that the game itself was ritualized; indeed, observers tell of its wild and frenzied play, anything but controlled and stylized. But its association in ritual contexts is strong. Archaeologists have excavated what they believe to be a large pit in which a ball post once stood from the ceremonial area of the Cemochechobee mound site in southern Georgia dating to about A.D. 1000. This would mean that the ancestors of the Creek Indians were playing ball in their sacred places. Thus, the presence of the single-pole game among the Seminoles is traceable at least to this period.

How widely spread the single-pole game was in the aboriginal Southeast is not known, but the Timucuans, with a language and culture very different from the proto-Creeks, were playing a form of it on the banks of the St. Johns River in Florida in the 1560s when observed by the Frenchman Le Moyne. This game was slightly different from the later Seminoles' game in that only young Timucuan men were allowed to play. But the care they took in erecting the pole, according to Le Moyne, and the way in which the game was played suggests some similarity of tradition, no matter what cultural variations existed. By the late seventeenth century, the ball game had become a metaphor of life for the Apalachee Indians of the Spanish mission province. A Franciscan priest recorded the Apalachee story that the ball game had been invented by one of their founding chiefs as a diversion to occupy a youth who he felt was destined to kill him and acquire his name.

Whatever its origins, when white men began writing about Seminole life and culture in the late 1800s they noticed that the ball game had a very definite role in the annual busk ceremony. Charles Barney Cory, writing in 1896, stated that the game was played on the afternoon of the first day. A photograph of this vintage shows the game under way at Pine Island at the eastern edge of the Everglades (fig. 5.5). The reasons the photographer kept his distance are understandable, but still we wish for a closer view. Some twenty years later, Alanson Skinner described two carved wooden ball sticks found at a camp he visited.

So the ball game was alive and well, passed down, we can surmise, from Mississippian cultures to the Creeks, to the Seminoles, and, after surviving the Seminole wars, to the near ancestors of today's Seminoles and Miccosukees. But again, until the work of Louis Capron in 1953, only the Indians themselves knew the full details of the game.

According to Capron, the ball pole was located just outside the dance circle and was a tall pine sapling twenty to twenty-five feet tall, with all

5.5. Seminole ball game at the Pine Island Green Corn dance grounds, photographed about 1897 by H. A. Ernst. (Reproduced with the permission of the Florida Anthropological Society and the Seminole Miccosukee Photographic Archives.)

branches but the topmost trimmed off. At a point about four to five feet above the ground, the pole was hewn square so that scores could be tallied in charcoal. As was the case elsewhere in the Southeast, the ball was made of deerskin stuffed with deer hair.

The game was played in the evenings of the busk or in the afternoon on Court Day. Boys had to use ball sticks to pick up and throw the ball, and girls had to use their hands. Teams were divided, boys against girls, and each side moved to one side of the pole or the other. The player first to have the ball threw it at the pole to try to hit it and the game went on from there. No holds were barred, and each player blocked, scuffled, pushed, and shoved trying to hit the pole with the ball. When the game was finished, the dance circle was swept clean by the medicine man's helpers.

Diversionary, yes, the game undoubtedly relieved mounting tensions pent up during the ritual season. Certainly it served to break the overall solemnity of the ceremony and, at least, acknowledged the energy of youth as a fact of life. That the game was played on sacred ground also suggests that the dual nature of human existence was recognized, that humans must exist with one another before dealing with the spirit world. Thus, in this view, one of the main functions of the game was to provide a sense of harmony and balance for human existence, secular and sacred together. Did the game function this way in prehistory, essentially as comic relief? Perhaps.

But the ball game did not have a universal meaning in the Americas. In Mesoamerica, where it was played in a formal walled court, the game was a ritual combat between warriors, the loser often vanquished to death. In the early Mississippian mound centers, the game may have existed in a similar context. Although its association appears to have been ceremonial during that period, we cannot say for certain that its function was identical to that later seen among the Seminoles. Although the Seminole busk undoubtedly reflected a selective, highly condensed version of complex Mississippian ceremonialism, it also contained elements unique to Seminole culture and history, elements given new meaning first by Creek society, then by the Seminoles. To understand the marvelous integration of sacred and secular, male and female, spontaneity and ritual shown by the Seminole ball game, we may not have to look beyond the Seminoles themselves.

The Hunting Dance

Although the annual busk ceremony was of central importance to the Florida Seminoles, a second ceremony took place in the fall, usually under a full moon between August and October. Unlike the annual busk, the Hunting Dance need only occur for four successive years. Also unlike the busk, the main concern of the Hunting Dance was not ritual purity and health and social harmony but to fend off potential harm done by snakes. This was done through the snakelike motions of the Snake Dance, in which both men and women participated, and by feasting, which provided a symbolic means for feeding the snake.

Again, the clan camps gathered at temporary camp sites, either at the busk grounds used previously or at a new location. Dances were held around the central fire at night, following an afternoon ball game. Every morning the men and boys hunted while the women gathered plant foods, and both prepared foods for the feast. For four days the routine was repeated. On the fifth day, the men left camp for the hunt; when they returned as late as seven days later the final feast was prepared. This involved the men giving strips of meat from the hunt to the women, who in turn passed to them loaves of corn bread baked while the men were away. Although protocol and ritual proscription of behavior were strong during the Hunting Dance for fear of offending the snake, overall the Hunting Dance did not have the seriousness of the busk, nor was the medicine involved.

Finally, there is yet another tantalizing link between recent Seminole ceremony and the beliefs and practices of the ancient Southeast. This is the mask ceremony, called the Old Man's Dance by Josie Billie in his discussion with William Sturtevant, danced perhaps for the last time around the turn of the twentieth century. Accounts from Oklahoma of similar vintage suggest that masks made of painted or stained tree bark or gourds were worn by old men in a dance that mimicked their victory over a dangerous animal in hunting. Although the specific meaning and function are obscure, one of the purposes of the ceremony was to scare young boys, perhaps as part of an initiation rite.

With the mention of masks we must immediately think of the military description of the Snake Warrior's village in 1842 mentioned in chapter 4 and the masks found there by the invading troops, and from this we must infer that the Seminole ceremonial repertoire during the Second Seminole War included the Old Man's Dance as well as the annual busk. The scene at Snake Warriors Island might be imagined: a masked figure bursts into the dance ring from the shadows with wild actions and growling shouts, scattering the young boys dancing there, grabbing one if he can, then returning to the darkness.

Beyond this, although the use of masks among the Creeks is not well documented, masking in other southeastern cultures was a widespread phenomenon of some antiquity, as the fabulous Key Marco specimens dramatically demonstrate. Masks among the Seminoles probably fulfilled the same broad functions of masks in other southeastern aboriginal cultures, or for that matter, cultures worldwide: the need to ease life's major transitions, the need to communicate with the spirit world and the realm of the ancestors, and the need to ritually transcend one's everyday identity.

That ceremonies and rituals were a major part of Seminole life through the recent historic past is confirmed by the combined evidence of archaeology, history, and oral tradition. That no modern ethnographer of the Seminoles knew and was fully aware of the depth and complexity of Seminole ceremonial life also cannot be denied. Some ceremonies, like the Old Man's Dance, vanished into obscurity before the outside world took an interest in appreciating rather than destroying Seminole culture. Other individual ceremonies may have been condensed or coalesced into the Green Corn Dance, or annual busk ceremony, under the harsh and stressful conditions brought on by the Seminole wars. The Second Seminole War in particular may have promoted a resurrection of certain dances having to do with a warrior's bravery and victory in battle. These dances and the activities associated with them, such as scalping, may have fallen into disuse when no longer needed. Although deeply linking the Seminoles to indigenous centuries-old traditions, the busks, bundles, and other aspects of Seminole religion and ritual were not static but continued to change and take on new form as the Seminoles themselves did.

6

Cows, Corn, and Coontie

↑ ↑ ↑ ↑ ↑ ↑ ↑ ↑ ↑ ↑ ↑ ↑

With the exception of an interesting but late development among the New River Seminoles of Biscayne Bay, the Seminoles were not a maritime people, nor was the focus of their food quest the biologically rich rivers, ponds, and wetlands of Florida. True, their villages were often located on the banks of rivers and streams, but this was mostly because these watery corridors of transportation connected them to each other and to the outside world. Florida rivers that now bear names given them by the Seminoles—the Withlacoochee, Wekiva, Oklawaha—were canoe highways for them, not sources of food. The Seminoles knew well that the prehistoric Indians of Florida had eaten oysters and other shellfish and left vast piles of shells behind to mark their former existence, but they also knew that this was not their way of life. Barfotartso, or "Old Charlie," told Charles Cory that the shellfish eaters were "Injuns all dead." Even coastal-dwelling Seminoles like those described by William Bartram in the 1770s living in the old Calusa area of Charlotte Harbor showed little interest in fishing for a living, instead engaging in a lively trade with the Cuban fishermen who frequented the area.

Early Seminole Farmers and Herders

The Seminoles came to Florida as farmers, herdsmen, and hunters. They did their best to preserve this basic way of making a living despite being pushed ever southward into the subtropics through the course of their history. The Seminoles came to Florida with the so-called American trilogy of their southeastern ancestors—corn, beans, and squash. They knew what it took to prepare the soil, plant the seeds, and harvest the crop so that their subsistence needs would be met. They knew what kind of soils their crops needed, much the same way a modern soil scientist can accurately guess what kinds of soils are to be found across the landscape, by seeing what kinds of trees grow there and how high above the nearest water source the land is.

Thus the Seminoles sought out the fertile hammock lands, well-drained rises or uplands supporting strong growths of oak. After clearing the trees from the center of the hammock, the Seminoles would then lay out their garden plots and build their houses nearby. The best hammocks were those surrounded by or close to prairies, seasonally wet grasslands where Seminole cattle could be turned loose to graze.

William Bartram described one such scene on his visit to Cowkeeper's Cuscowilla Seminoles near present-day Paynes Prairie. In this case, the fields were planted "on the rich prolific lands" on the rim of the great Alachua savanna about two miles from the village. Here grew corn, Indian potato, at least five types of squash (one perhaps the curious Seminole "hanging" pumpkin), and a tropical viny legume identified by Bartram as a member of the Dolichos family (probably a type of pea). Everyone in the village played a part in keeping the crops healthy until they could be harvested. At night, men patrolled the field to keep nocturnal predators at bay, deer, raccoons, and bears being as fond then as now of the sweet plants people grow. During the day guard duty was shifted to children and the elderly, whose main task was to drive away nuisance birds. The field itself was divided into family plots, with all people helping in the planting and tending until time for harvest. At harvest, each family would take from their own plot and contribute some portion to the common stores. Each family's food supply was also supplemented by small dooryard gardens kept at their dwellings, in which smaller amounts of corn, beans, and tobacco were grown. Each family also planted citrus trees near their house garden, where they could be watched and picked with little effort (the modern archaeologist searching for former Seminole village sites learns to look for stands of sour orange trees to mark these locations!).

Below the fields on the vast prairie wandered the herds of Seminole cattle, looked after by Seminoles on horseback. Bartram was pleased by the appearance of the cattle, as fat as any he had seen in Pennsylvania, and later was well satisfied with the barbecued ribs presented him by Cowkeeper. He was less enthralled with a tripe soup made from the entrails of the animals, no matter how well seasoned, but noted that the Indians held it to be a delicacy. Not of a culture prone to waste, the Seminoles made highly efficient use of the cow, entrail soup aside. Horns were used to hold powder for their muskets. Stretched skins were used during the Second Seminole War to make skin boats capable of moving from island to island in the

Central Florida Lake Tsala Apopka chain. Tons of jerked beef were prepared by Indians during this same period as provision for life on the run.

Because the Spanish cattle ranch of La Chua once operated on the north rim of the Alachua savanna in the years before the Seminoles came, it is natural to think that Cowkeeper's Seminoles learned the intricacies of cattle herding by taking over the nearly feral animals left behind after La Chua's demise. But there are indications that cattle were present among the Creeks by the 1730s (along with pigs and chickens), prior to Cowkeeper's migration to Florida. By 1764 the Creek chief Wolf King managed two hundred head of black cattle, made fat by feasting on the cane swamps of the Tallapoosa River. Thus, Cowkeeper's Seminoles may already have known about cattle, valued them, and found their presence to be a compelling reason to settle the former La Chua range. At the very least, the Seminole cowboy of today can trace the history of his profession back some two hundred years.

Cattle, horses, and hogs were to become measures of a Seminole's wealth. Horses, like cattle, were derived from the Spanish stock and were raised, bred, and traded to great advantage by the Seminoles. Frontier ruffians and outlaws such as the notorious "McGirt gang" often preyed on herds of Seminole horses, challenging the colonial authorities and the Seminoles themselves to retaliate for their thievery. When Payne, Cowkeeper's nephew, assumed leadership of the Alachua band, raising animals and raising crops were no longer simply a means of survival but were looked upon as a way of obtaining both cash and supplies in the colonial trade economy. Packhorse trains moved from interior Seminole plantations to St. Augustine or to trading spots on the St. Johns or Suwannee rivers, laden with corn, potatoes, peaches, and rice. Along the St. Johns and other rivers moved Seminole canoes carrying melons, potatoes, oranges, and honey. Oranges and peaches probably were carryovers from the Spanish mission fields and, like Spanish cattle, were quickly seized upon by the Seminoles for their trade value. The melons mentioned by Bartram, if they were watermelons, may also have mission origins, as watermelon seeds have been found in excavations at seventeenth-century Florida mission sites.

The use of honey by the Seminoles provides a more curious example of the opportunities provided them in Florida. Honeybees are not native to North America and were shipped across the Atlantic to the Virginia Colony and to New England in the early 1600s to provide a reliable source of honey for the colonists (the role played by bees in crop pollination not being recognized until at least a century later). Swarms of honeybees from these domestic hives rapidly swept west, reaching the Mississippi River by 1800.

Perhaps they moved south as well, finding hollow trees in the Florida wet-lands to their liking. Perhaps hives were introduced by the British who established themselves on St. Johns River plantations by the 1770s. What-ever the origin of the bees, their honey was used by the Seminoles to sweeten oranges, to mix with flour made from the smilax root to make a sweet jelly, and to fill deerskin bags for trade with the whites for items such as sewing needles and fishhooks.

How and when rice came to the Seminoles is not known exactly. Some scholars argue that escaped African slaves brought the knowledge of rice cultivation with them into Florida and shared it with their Seminole allies. This is believable but undocumented. Rice was said by Bartram to be present among the Seminoles in the 1770s, planted in hills on dry ground, so Creek origins (by way of English planters in Georgia) might be indicated. But rice cultivation was also well suited to the wet prairies and wetland margins sought out by the Seminoles as their cattle herds increased. The Black Seminoles, hidden even deeper in the Central Florida swamps, would have seen the growing of rice as a logical use of this environment. They also readily adopted the use of sugarcane and were known to have cultivated dense stands of this crop in the Withlacoochee River wetlands. By the early decades of the 1800s, rice had become an established element of the Seminole agricultural economy.

Rice had many benefits to offer the Seminoles as an item of trade. It could be grown and harvested relatively easily in large quantities and could be stored or stockpiled for long periods of time. Rice is nonperishable and could be transported across long distances in rough conditions with little or no loss. Spanish St. Augustine, always hungry, valued the steady supply of staple foods brought in by Seminole farmers of the Central Florida bread-basket. Horse caravans arriving in St. Augustine were noted by colonial authorities. Despite its importance in Seminole trade, rice seems to have had far less impact on the Seminole diet.

Going to the Coontie Grounds

Although the Seminoles were adept at growing domesticated plants such as corn and rice, wild plant foods continued to provide a major part of their subsistence needs. The importance of wild foods may have increased dur-ing the war years, particularly after 1835, and no doubt these plants were relied upon to make the successful adaptation to the subtropical environ-ment of South Florida. But even when the Seminoles were growing corn and other vegetables on Everglades and Big Cypress tree islands, finding and collecting wild plant foods remained important activities. Families or entire bands would move to the coontie grounds, setting up temporary camps there for the duration of the harvest. Important coontie grounds existed in the hammocks of the Pine Island chain on the eastern edge of the Everglades and the uplands northwest of Lake Okeechobee. In a letter to Colonel William Worth dated June 7, 1842, naval commander John T. McLaughlin listed the routing of women and children from the coontie grounds in the Little River and Arch Creek areas west of Biscayne Bay as one of his major accomplishments.

Coontie, from the Mikasuki word *konti*, is prepared from the root of the tropical cycad *Zamia*. According to anthropologist William Sturtevant, the word *konti* was once used by both Mikasuki and Creek speakers to refer to the smilax plant, an evergreen thorny vine with a large potatolike starchy root used by the North Florida Seminoles in a variety of dishes. Both smilax and *Zamia* roots require rather elaborate processing to make them edible. Because the early Seminoles in North Florida knew how to prepare smilax roots, the later use of *Zamia* in South Florida is thought by many to have been a continuation of this adaptation. Others think that the particular Seminole technology of zamia processing reflects interaction with the West Indies, where similar practices existed.

The resemblance between the Seminole techniques of processing smilax and *Zamia* are compelling. Seminoles living on the Suwannee River in the late 1700s chopped the smilax roots into small pieces, pounded them thoroughly in a wooden mortar to the consistency of coarse flour, then mixed the root flour in a tray with clean water. This mixture was strained into a second container through several basket sieves. The sediment that formed in the bottom of this second container was allowed to air-dry, resulting in what was said to be a fine reddish meal. From this meal a kind of jelly was made by adding warm water and honey or, when mixed with corn flour and fried in bear's oil, the meal combined to make hot cakes.

In less than fifty years the Seminoles would no longer be the rulers of the Suwannee, plying its long course in their sturdy dugout canoes, entertaining traders and frontier diplomats as they passed back and forth between St. Augustine, St. Marks, and the Creek country. The raids of the Georgians, then Jackson and his Tennesseans, and finally U.S. army regulars and volunteers would drive the Seminoles south, from the rivers, prairies, and hammocks that had originally attracted them to Florida, to a terrain and geography with which they were less familiar. In anthropological terms, this move from north to south, from temperate to true subtropical conditions, has been understood as an adaptive shift, a cultural response necessary to survive in the face of new and challenging environmental circumstances.

The chickee is perhaps the most readily identifiable symbol of this adaptive shift. The substantial log or board houses typical of Seminole dwellings in the north and central peninsula were abandoned in favor of the open-air, raised-floor chickee as the Seminoles experienced the hot humid conditions of South Florida. More subtle changes occurred in every aspect of Seminole culture, including settlement patterns, political organization, religion, and economy, each reflecting both increasing social isolation and reliance on widely dispersed natural resources.

The Seminole use of coontie as a food source shows that this adaptive shift involved the application of traditional technologies to new circumstances. The basic sieving technique used by the Seminoles to process smilax roots was adapted for the production of coontie flour. By the time careful observations were made of the Seminoles making coontie flour in 1880, the process was much more elaborate than that used for smilax and may have reflected some degree of outside influence. Indeed, by this time whites in South Florida were making coontie flour in factories for the commercial market. But it also seems logical to conclude that the early processing of coontie, in the 1830s and 1840s (in the coontie grounds sought after by the U.S. military), reflected a direct continuity with the earlier smilax technology, however basic.

We must rely on Clay MacCauley's account of his 1880 visit to the Seminoles temporarily encamped at the coontie grounds at Horse Creek, near present-day Haines City, for our first glimpse of the Seminole process of coontie making. The roots were first gathered and washed, sometimes by the children, then chopped and placed in the coontie log, a long pine log with holes cut in it to serve as mortars (fig. 6.1). Wooden pestles were then used to pulverize the roots into a pulpy mass, which was laid on a small platform, placed in a small bark basket, and saturated with water from the creek.

The next step was to strain the pulp through a cloth into a deerskin suspended below (fig. 6.2). Here the starchy water was left to ferment for several days, then spread on palmetto leaves to dry. The coontie flour was then ready to be kneaded into dough to make a bread that, in MacCauley's words, was not unpleasant to the taste. What coontie bread lacked in taste it made up for in reliability, as it was an important dietary staple when the Seminoles' planted crops failed or were ravaged by animals. The Seminoles

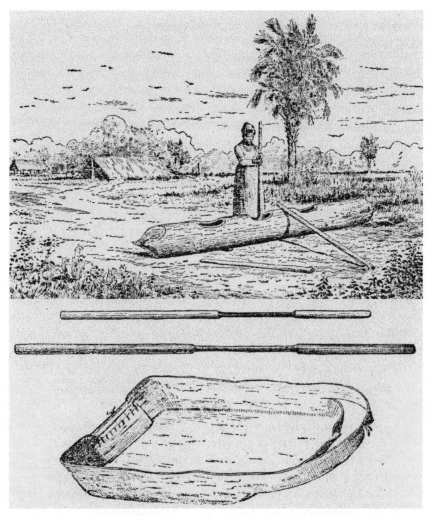

6.1. Coontie log, pestles, and mash vessel, used by the Seminoles in 1880. From MacCauley's 1887 Smithsonian report.

had learned never to rely solely on garden crops in South Florida. Too much water, too little water, soil too wet or dry, high winds or uncontrollable acts of nature, and marauding beasts all could take their toll on the plantings at a moment's notice. Besides coontie, other wild foods counted on by the Seminoles were the new shoots of the cabbage palmetto, eaten cooked or raw, and the wild potato.

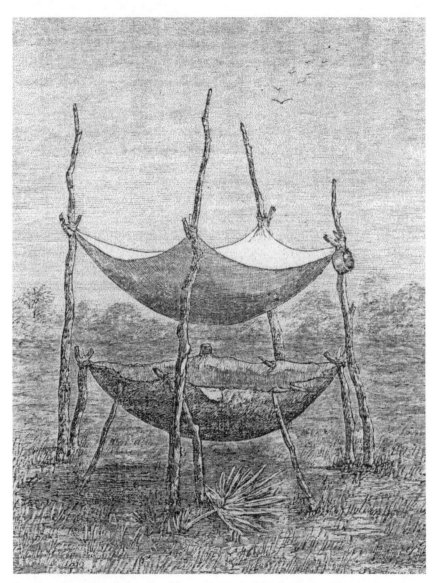

6.2. Coontie strainer in use in 1880, as shown in MacCauley's 1887 report.

The Curious Case of the Seminole Banana

The most exotic element in the Seminole garden was the banana. In a relatively short period of time, bananas achieved a unique association with the Seminoles in South Florida, well beyond their limited contribution to the diet. Eventually, a Seminole tourist village in Miami, Musa Isle, was named after the scientific name of the plant. The word *musa* comes from the Arabic word *mouz*, is referred to in the Koran as the "Tree of Paradise," and derives from Sanskrit. Ultimately by the 1950s the Seminoles would know of or cultivate at least five varieties of bananas, including the original "horse" banana. Some say the destruction of Billy Bowlegs' banana patch by U.S. soldiers helped trigger the Third Seminole War in 1855. How did the Seminoles get bananas, and why were bananas important to them?

Bananas were seen in St. Augustine in the 1760s, perhaps introduced by the Spanish who brought them to the Caribbean from the Canary Islands as early as 1516. By the seventeenth century, banana cultivation had spread throughout the West Indies. Thus two sources of Seminole bananas are possible—through a West Indies connection, undocumented but certainly not impossible, or through St. Augustine. Either way, anthropologist William Sturtevant's guess that the Seminole word for banana, *wilantana*, is derived from the Spanish *platano* cannot be ruled out.

The first documentary evidence we have for the Seminole use of bananas comes from Second Seminole War military documents. Writing on May 26, 1842, a naval officer reports the destruction in the vicinity of Snake Creek of an island field of untended crops, including bananas, by troops pursuing the Seminoles into the Everglades. Then there is the famous Billy Bowlegs incident of 1855.

Tensions between white and Seminole had built once again, and the pressure was on to complete the removal of the Indians left undone at the close of the Second Seminole War in 1842. Violent incidents spurred retaliations by both sides, leaving several dead and wounding the dream that the Seminoles would be left to live in peace. Through the early 1850s, Billy Bowlegs was wooed with trips to Baltimore, Philadelphia, and New York, but he steadfastly refused any agreement to leave Florida permanently for Indian Territory. A military solution was embraced by Secretary of War Jefferson Davis and, late in 1855, troop build-ups began at posts along the lower Florida coasts.

A reconnaissance patrol led by Lieutenant George Hartsuff was ordered to the interior, moving southeast into the Big Cypress from Fort Myers. When his men found the abandoned village of Billy Bowlegs on December

18, they pillaged it and, according to a later account, hacked down his banana trees and took the bananas. This act, some claim, particularly inflamed Bowlegs, who attacked the party two days later, killing and wounding several. Hartsuff himself suffered wounds to the arm, chest, and stomach but managed to escape.

Although Billy Bowlegs' bananas cannot be held solely responsible for the resulting Third Seminole War (1855–1858), the story does suggest that bananas may have had some importance to Bowlegs and his Seminoles beyond their role as a food source. Even in this regard there is some question as to why the Seminoles would bother growing them. Each plant produces relatively low yield and must be cut down to regrow to produce its next crop. Once harvested, bananas ripen quickly and are perishable, not easily stored for long periods of time. Further, they seem not to have entered the Seminole cuisine in any significant way, as did plantains in Caribbean cultures.

Could it be that bananas had some prestige value for the Seminoles? Perhaps bananas were offered to visitors or guests, as Bartram had been feasted with barbecue and honey by Cowkeeper and the White King. Perhaps, because they were exotic, bananas were a symbol of a man's connection to the outside world, his worldliness. Perhaps a family's garden simply was not considered complete without its stand of bananas. Whatever the case, by the early 1900s bananas were considered by outside observers to be regular features of the Seminole landscape.

The Technology of the Seminole Food Quest

The functional simplicity of Seminole Indian technology relating to the food quest belies the fundamental elegance of its adaptiveness. Left to speak for themselves, the elements of Seminole material culture tell of functional minimalism, of forms designed to do work and accomplish tasks with maximum efficiency, minimal effort. What could be done without technological elaboration was. Artifacts tell us of continuity with the past, of conservatism, of forms hard won and slow to change.

One can easily imagine the small open bowls found by archaeologists in the Suwannee River being used to serve William Bartram china-briar root soup (made from the smilax root), or perhaps the beef tripe about which he so eloquently complained. These bowls are shaped to be held comfortably in one's hands or resting in one's lap. Probably made of local Suwannee River clay containing sand and particles of limestone, the pots were deco-

6.3. Wooden mortar found near the
Sawgrass Mills mall, Broward County.
(Photograph courtesy of the Archaeo-
logical and Historical Conservancy.)

rated with incised lines and ticks around their carinated shoulders that
came directly from the ancestral Creek tradition (see fig. 1.5).

Broken pottery sherds preserve well in the archaeological record and are
studied endlessly by archaeologists. But wood preserves less well, sadly,
because wood was certainly a major element of Seminole subsistence technology. One reads tantalizing accounts in old newspapers of the discovery
by some pioneer or homesteader of wooden mortars, pestles, or other
equipment in long-abandoned Seminole camps, but the present whereabouts of most of these items is unknown and cannot be traced. Rarely, such
specimens come to light, like the wooden mortar found by a backhoe opera-
tor during the construction of the Sawgrass Mills mall in Broward County.
This piece weighs twenty pounds, is fourteen inches deep, and was reported to be of cypress wood (fig. 6.3). A mortar of this type may have been
used to pound corn with the help of a double-ended wooden pestle, one
end rectangular and blunt, the other pointed (fig. 6.4). Other wooden mortars were V-shaped or tapered, designed to be transported in canoes.

However, the tools and equipment used by the Seminoles for obtaining
food and preparing it should not be thought of as being strictly expedient
or interchangeable. The mortar and pestle used for grinding corn would not
do for pulverizing coontie roots. The two-part bark vessel made for sieving

6.4. Mortar and pestle for grinding corn, 1880. From MacCauley's 1887 Smithsonian report.

coontie mash was different in form and function from the shallow, open-weave pottery basket used for sifting corn.

Nor should Seminole attitudes toward technology be thought of as so conservative as to prevent the seizing of new opportunities. New technologies could be quickly developed or adopted when called for. Presented with an abundance of manatees in the New River and Biscayne Bay, local Seminoles went after them with canoes, steel-tipped harpoons, and floats all specially designed for the purpose. Naturalist and sportsman Charles Barney Cory claimed to have often accompanied the Seminoles on manatee hunts. Standing poised in a long, broad canoe, hunters at the bow and stern would keep their eyes peeled for surfacing manatees as a youth or another man carefully guided them along with a paddle. When a manatee was spotted, a harpoon point, attached to a rope and float, was thrust deeply into the shoulder or neck of the animal. Although the manatee would dive or swim away, its movements were marked by the float. The Seminoles would follow the float, wait for the manatee to surface again, and then shoot it in the head. The manatee would then be towed to shore behind the canoe by means of the float rope. According to Cory, the Seminoles kept as much of the meat as they could eat and sold the rest to their white neighbors.

The manatee hunting practiced by the New River Seminoles shows considerable refinement over the more opportunistic hunting done by the Suwannee River Seminoles of Talahasochte in the 1770s. On the banks of Manatee Springs, William Bartram saw the skeleton of a manatee killed by the Seminoles during the previous winter. Although we do not know exactly how this animal was killed, it was most probably spotted in the crystal clear waters of the spring run and speared from the bank or the cypress at

6.5. Rope Cypress shooting with bow and arrow from canoe, Florida Everglades. (Courtesy American Museum of Natural History, Deptartment of Library Services, #48140.)

the water's edge. The discovery of sea cows, or "giant beavers" as the Seminoles called them, in the waters of the Suwannee was certainly a bonus for the Talahasochte Seminoles and may have become the basis for knowledge passed down from generation to generation. Just as the early use of smilax later may have made the benefits of processing coontie easy to recognize, so the early use of manatee as a food source may have entered the cultural memory bank of the Seminoles. Yet it could be also that the New River Seminoles simply recognized a good thing when they saw it and pulled together the tools, weapons, and ingenuity needed to accomplish the task. Such was the nature of adaptation and change in Seminole culture. Rarely flashy or embellished, their technology nonetheless rose to meet the occasion, using what worked of the old ways, bringing in the new as needed.

7

Patchwork and Polyester

Seminoles and Miccosukees in the Modern World

↑ ↑ ↑ ↑ ↑ ↑ ↑ ↑ ↑ ↑ ↑ ↑

By the early years of the twentieth century, the problem with the Seminoles became clear. They were not going to go away (fig. 7.1). Neither was the white man. How were the Indians to live as Indians in a white man's world? This is where complications arose, because there was no single answer to this question, no single shared or unanimous vision among the Seminoles for how to live in a world that they did not control. If there was to be one certain truth of Florida Indian reality in the twentieth century, it was this. There was not to be one tribe, one people. In a sense, history could have told us this. The term *Seminole*, as broadly applied, glossed a considerable amount of cultural diversity, with considerable time depth in the aboriginal Southeast.

Certainly, as broadly applied, the term *Seminole* implied a level of ethnic identity that may have been more imagined than real. Throughout the years of the Second Seminole War (1835–1842), it was common for outside observers to refer to the Indian foe not as Seminole only but additionally and more specifically as Mikasuki (or variations thereof), Tallahassee or Tallasay, Creek, and others. We have seen in chapter 3 how the stresses of the war years helped forge a unique cultural identity for the Seminoles, a shared identity that encouraged the various bands to interact with one another. But the strong impulse to live one's life within the social reality of the family and band or lineage group remained. Added to this was the noted tendency in Seminole society to tolerate, if not encourage, individualistic, nonconformist behavior. Clay MacCauley, Robert Pratt, Hugh Willoughby, and others who traveled among the Seminoles in the latter part of the nineteenth century all remarked on individual Seminoles who did things differently, their own way, often adapting the customs of the outside world to suit their own purposes. The tendencies of individualism and a preference for

7.1. Wilson Cypress, 1910, photographed by Julian Dimock for anthropologist Alanson Skinner. (Courtesy of the American Museum of Natural History, Special Collections, #48195.)

kin-based relations, clearly seen in the Seminoles of the nineteenth century, would have significant consequences for Seminole life in the century ahead.

Twentieth-century pressures on the Seminoles also were very different from those in the previous century of conflict and hostility. The government no longer wanted to exterminate the Seminoles or enforce their captivity. But beyond that a clear Indian policy was difficult to discern. Through the decades of the twentieth century the pendulum would swing between the belief that the Seminoles should take their part in modern Florida society like any other citizens, leaving their past behind, giving up their Indian identity, to the notion that the Seminoles had the right to exist as a sovereign nation, apart from but somehow coexisting with state and federal governments. There could be no single Seminole response to the inevitable uncertainties of twentieth-century political reality nor to the overwhelming complexities of twentieth-century life. They were no longer fighting for their lives but rather to make their way in the modern world. That there now exist two federally recognized tribes—the Seminoles and the Miccosukees—and a third group of Independents again illustrates that the Indians chose more than one path of survival.

New Ways of Life

By the 1890s the Seminoles understood that they would no longer be able to live in isolation (fig. 7.2). Some had sought on their own to break the isolation and had traveled to Orlando and Fort Myers to walk the streets and observe this new and exotic society. Others were busy exchanging otter pelts, egret plumes, deer hides, and alligator skins with trading stores around Biscayne Bay (fig. 7.3). But, with increasing frequency since the 1880s, the outside world was coming to them, penetrating their sanctuary in the Everglades and Big Cypress on foot, by boat, even by ox-drawn wagon. On the heels of the sportsmen came the so-called visionaries, those who dreamed of transforming the watery wilderness of the Everglades into a terra firma capable of supporting large-scale agriculture and new settlement. Soon, the Seminoles found themselves enmeshed in the global economy, as they had been one hundred and fifty years earlier with the deerskin trade. But then global circumstances lessened the demand for hides and pelts as World War I swirled, and it became illegal to hunt the plume birds. Soon after entering the modern world, the Seminoles became

7.2. Seminoles inspecting artifacts collected by Skinner, 1910. (Courtesy of the American Museum of Natural History, Special Collections, #48210.)

7.3. Skinning an alligator. Photograph by Julian Dimock. (Courtesy of the American Museum of Natural History, Special Collections, #48178.)

its victims. By the time the Great Depression slammed the rest of the country in 1929, the Seminoles already had long endured economic hard times.

Economic rescue came at first not from government relief but rather from an unexpected source. The automobile came to South Florida, first across the Tamiami Trail in 1928, carrying loads of cultural tourists eager for vicarious escape into another world. The highway, constructed at a rate of about one and one-fourth miles per month, had taken five years to complete and crossed seven counties for a distance of 273 miles. Within ten years, as many as thirteen Seminole families had moved out of the Big Cypress or Miami tourist camps to roadside villages, among them the families of Robert Billie at Weaver's Station, Harley Jumper at Royal Palm Hammock, Josie Billie at Ochopee, and William McKinley Osceola east of the Forty-Mile Bend. For a small fee, tourists could enter the family compound, watch the matriarch or her daughters sew patchwork or weave baskets, and have the opportunity to buy these crafts directly from their makers. For the Trail Seminoles, some of whom would later organize as the Miccosukee Tribe, tourist economics allowed them to survive while doing what they did best, and a new way of life was born.

Tourist camps in Miami, some established as early as 1917, also allowed the Seminoles to be economically independent and largely free from government interference. True, the attractions were not owned by Seminoles, but camp residents received wages, food, and the opportunity to earn extra cash in a setting generally free from overt exploitation. Patchwork art reached a florescence during this period, as demand increased and women spent more time perfecting their skills. By the 1930s, the Musa Isle Indian Village had become an established fixture on the Miami tourist scene and had become the place to go if one wanted to see the Indians in their native element, such as wrestling alligators. Despite the addition of such new activities, the tourist villages essentially remained matrilineal clan camps, organized along lines of female descent as the Seminoles and their ancestors had been for centuries.

The success of the attractions in the end helped contribute to their demise. The government was eager to extend its New Deal to the Seminoles, difficult to do if they did not need it. A government agent, Roy Nash, spoke strongly against the camps, condemning their pitiful and demoralizing conditions and what he saw as a dead-end economy. Although expressing sympathy for the plight of the Seminoles and writing of his admiration for their ability to adapt to the challenging South Florida environment, Nash saw the future of the Seminoles as being firmly within the protective hands of the government. A second agent, Gene Stirling, wrote even more vehemently against the camps in 1935. Others, professing to be friends of the Seminoles, felt the same way.

The Seminoles themselves were divided on the issue of government support, one of several crucial issues in the 1930s that split Seminole society and forced them to take sides. Beginning in 1894, the federal government purchased land in South Florida to be used as a Seminole reservation, with large areas later added by the State of Florida. But no Indians lived on these lands. Why should they? The land itself was no more or less appealing than the existing locations of the Seminoles. But, in the absence of government programs, there were simply no incentives to move. The Indian New Deal changed that, and for the first time, services, programs, and land were brought together in a systematic effort to "train" the Seminoles for self-sufficiency. As government programs took hold at Dania, west of Fort Lauderdale, and at Big Cypress in Hendry County, Seminole families began to move to these reservations. Others tenaciously clung to their roadside villages along the Tamiami Trail and resisted government contact with increasing fervor.

A New God

As more Seminoles moved on to the new reservations at Big Cypress and Dania, Baptist missionaries were soon to follow. Many Seminoles were converted, and churches were built. One hundred and fifty years earlier, Cowkeeper's Seminoles had captive Christian Indians among them, the mission Yamasees from Spanish Florida. Now, the Seminoles were becoming Christians themselves. The reservations became places where Christian Seminoles lived; those who preferred traditional native religion stayed along the Tamiami Trail. Dedicated and effective, the missionaries preached in the Muskogee language and used Muskogee texts, taking advantage of the fact that Muskogee was used as a political common tongue among both Muskogee-speaking and Mikasuki-speaking Seminoles.

Christianity, at least as practiced by the Seminoles, did not necessarily require a complete rejection of traditional beliefs. Some Seminoles adopted aspects of Christianity that did not directly contradict the old ways and were not rigid or dogmatic about their beliefs. This was possible in part because elements of Christianity already had infiltrated aboriginal religion centuries before and had become part of the "old ways." When anthropologist Merwyn Garbarino lived on the Big Cypress reservation in the mid-1960s, she observed that some attended weekly church services for their social and political contacts rather than to demonstrate their faith. Others rejected Christianity, saying that the Christian God was not unlike the Master of Breath and thus offered nothing new. For the traditionals, the Green Corn Dance was the ultimate ritual experience and was vital to their very existence. Busk groups persisted and the Green Corn Dance continued, despite the successes of the Baptist Church. But by the late 1940s Christianity had gained a strong foothold among the Seminoles and has increased in importance in the fifty years since.

Not all missionaries lived on the reservations. For one of these, Deaconess Harriet Bedell, overt religious conversion was not even the primary goal. First working with the Blanket Cheyenne in Oklahoma between 1905 and 1915 and with Athabascans in Alaska from 1915 until 1932, the deaconess arrived in Florida with the aim of stimulating an arts and crafts industry among the Seminoles to encourage economic self-sufficiency. The Seminoles gave her a cold reception and refused to have much to do with her for several years. But this "small steam engine in petticoats," in Marjory Stoneman Douglas's words, was not to be put off and was able to establish the Glades Cross Mission in Everglades City. Here, Seminoles who lived along the Tamiami Trail or in Everglades camps began to bring baskets, miniature carved boats, dolls, aprons, blouses, sofkee spoons, and other items for sale to retailers and the tourist trade. For this she took nothing in return, only the satisfaction in doing what she thought was best for the Seminoles.

On at least one occasion, however, Bedell overstepped her limits with the Seminoles, harming rather than helping her cause. On September 13, 1946, the *Miami Herald* carried the story of how the Episcopalian deaconess usurped Baptist preacher (and Oklahoma Creek) Stanley Smith's funeral service for Jimmie Osceola. Jimmie Osceola was reported to be ninety-five years old at the time of his death, the last survivor of the Seminole wars. Apparently unsatisfied with Smith's service, Deaconess Bedell conducted her own impromptu graveside ceremony devoid of native practices, according to the newspaper account. Some Seminoles were visibly agitated by her behavior, and one remarked that the deaconess had only added to their "great burden of grief." Undaunted, Deaconess Harriet Bedell carried on at the Glade Cross Mission until her retirement in 1962 at age eighty-six.

Reservation Life

Today members of the Seminole Tribe live on reservations at Hollywood, Big Cypress, Brighton, Tampa, Immokalee, and Fort Pierce. Most Miccosukees live within the five-mile, five-hundred-foot-wide reservation centered on the Forty-Mile Bend of the Tamiami Trail (fig. 7.4). Reservation lands are held in trust for the Seminoles and Miccosukees by the U.S. government and thus are not completely free from federal control. The Seminole Tribe in particular has purchased reservation lands in areas reflecting historical use and has used these properties to launch business ventures. In 1981, eight and a half acres on Orient Road in east Tampa were purchased as a place to reinter the Seminole burials unearthed beneath the city's Fort Brooke parking garage. A hotel and restaurant, bingo hall, and tax-free cigarette shop soon followed.

Locations of early Seminole settlements in the Florida panhandle such as John Hicks' Town near Madison have also been considered potential reservation sites. Leading this charge is Seminole Tribal Chairman James Billie, who rightly sees the irony in the Seminoles' ability to buy back lands that once were theirs. In 1996, fifty acres of pine flatwoods west of Fort Pierce in St. Lucie County became the sixth Seminole reservation and will be home to Seminole families who have deep roots in the area.

Reservations have always been important as locations where government programs and the ways of the outside world could be introduced to

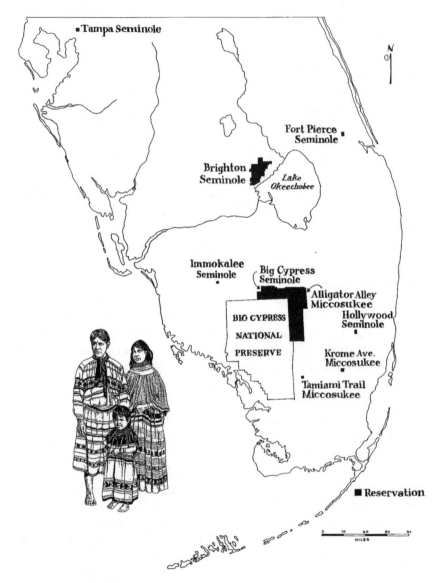

Tampa Seminole

Fort Pierce Seminole

Brighton Seminole

Lake Okeechobee

Immokalee Seminole

Big Cypress Seminole

Alligator Alley Miccosukee

BIG CYPRESS NATIONAL PRESERVE

Hollywood Seminole

Krome Ave. Miccosukee

Tamiami Trail Miccosukee

N

■ **Reservation**

0 10 20 20 40
MILES

7.4. Seminole and Miccosukee reservations in Florida. (Drawn by Theodore Morris, reproduced with the artist's permission.)

the Seminoles, and reservation lands were being acquired as early as 1891. Not until the 1930s did the Seminoles begin to move on to reservation lands in any numbers, showing the same reluctance their ancestors expressed when forced to move within the bounds of the Central Florida reservation following the Treaty of Moultrie Creek in 1823. A combination of social services, missionary activity, and the harsh economic reality of 1930s life off the reservation were sufficient enticement for those Seminoles who chose to move within the reservation boundaries. The government-sponsored cattle program that eventually took hold at Brighton and Big Cypress provided some economic incentive. Having overcome many serious obstacles, including poor natural grazing lands, improper breed selection of the original stock, lack of training, government loan burdens, and the transition to private ownership of the herds, the modern Seminole cowboy deals in the high-tech world of satellite cattle sales, with images beamed to prospective buyers throughout the southern and western states.

The Seminole and Miccosukee reservations strive to be self-sufficient communities, each with its own identity. Although the individual reservations are strongly connected to the central tribal government in political, economic, and social ways, and to one another by people who marry in or out or move back and forth, each has taken on its own unique personality based on its environmental setting and history. The Hollywood reservation very much resembles any modern suburban community on the outskirts of any American city, with the exception that many of the modest concrete-block houses have chickees in their backyards. Brighton, sitting on the prairies above Lake Okeechobee, has the look and feel of a rural ranch community, not unlike hundreds of other rural hamlets spread across the country. Big Cypress feels like a world apart, a place not of this century, a land where humans and nature exist in a primal relationship. The Billie Swamp Safari and Camping Village, a 2,000-acre attraction on the reservation, opened in 1993 in the hope that the Big Cypress ambience would prove to be a marketable commodity. Ecotourists can ride swamp buggies, airboats, or canoes through the "land where the legendary Seminoles retreated from the Seminole Wars" (to quote the brochure); eat catfish, gator tail, or frog legs at the Swamp Water Café; watch a sunset; and camp at an authentic chickee village. The Miccosukee Reservation on the Forty-Mile Bend is precariously perched on the edge of the Everglades, hanging on to the shoulder of the Tamiami Trail, balanced between past and present.

The reservations have their own police force, and the established reservations also have their own schools, clinics, libraries, community centers, and recreational facilities. No longer just locations where government control can be extended over the Indian people, the reservations today are providing a focal point for the renewed tribal emphasis on traditional Indian values and cultural heritage. Although originally developed by the government to acculturate the Indians, the reservations exist today because the Seminoles want them to. Tribal Chairman James Billie's efforts alone led to the doubling of the Seminole reservations between 1979 and 1996. The reservations are strongly intertwined with the economic viability of both tribes and deeply embedded in the social and cultural identities of their Indian residents. It is difficult to imagine an Indian future without the reservations.

Two Nations

The Indians known historically as the Seminoles are today divided into two federally recognized tribes, the Seminole Tribe of Florida with more than two thousand members, and the Miccosukee Tribe of Indians of Florida with about six hundred members. A third group, known as the Independents, number about one hundred and share the history and culture of the Seminoles and Miccosukees but have chosen not to enroll in those tribes. The Seminole Tribe is governed by a council of elected representatives from the three largest reservations and a tribal chairman and has a separate corporate board of directors who manage the many business interests of the tribe. The Miccosukee Tribe has a similar division of power between a tribal council, consisting of an elected chairman and all members of the tribe over the age of eighteen, and an elected business council who oversee the tribe's corporate ventures. Both tribes are federally recognized, the Seminoles since 1957, the Miccosukees since 1962, which means, ostensibly at least, that the federal government recognizes them as sovereign nations and must therefore deal with the Seminoles and Miccosukees on a nation-to-nation basis.

However, Indian sovereignty in actual practice is complex, certainly conditional, and continually subject to renegotiation as municipal, state, and federal governments react to the Indians' attempt to act as autonomous nations. It was one thing to recognize Indian sovereignty when they were just "selling trinkets by the side of the road" (to quote Tribal Chairman James Billie in an interview with the *Orlando Sentinel* on June 1, 1986), quite another when the Indians are seeking authority to run casino gambling, raffles, horse and dog racing, jai alai, and other forms of gaming. The stakes are very high for both sides. Bingo and gaming can bring the Seminoles and Miccosukees out of the past and provide an economic foundation for a diversity of business enterprises. By the 1980s, up to 65 percent of the Seminole tribal budget was derived from bingo proceeds and the sale of tax-free cigarettes. But should the Indians be allowed to offer casino gambling and other forms of gaming that the state deems illegal and prohibited under current state law? As sovereign nations, do the tribes have the right to sue the state in their quest to open casinos? The federal government says yes, under the provisions of the Indian Gaming Regulatory Act, but only if the state has failed to negotiate the issue with the tribes in good faith. In 1995, the question went to the Supreme Court, where the Seminoles challenged the state's right to control Indian gaming. This contentious issue is a long way from being resolved and will likely be battled over for years to come. As it stands at present, the Indians are allowed to offer only types of gaming considered permissible by the state. This would appear, for the moment, to form a working definition of the limits of Indian sovereignty. Land use, water rights, and the use of endangered species such as the panther for traditional religious purposes also create flash points in the sovereignty equation.

In an earlier time, government policies were in part responsible for the political division between the Seminoles and Miccosukees. After years of funding government support to the reservation Seminoles through social service and agricultural programs, the U.S. Congress began considering the "termination" of the Indians from such support in the early 1950s, thinking that it was time that the Indians made their way into mainstream society. After all, some entrepreneurial Seminoles already had demonstrated their ability to function successfully in the white man's world. If they could do it, then it could be done. Thus the Seminoles quickly found themselves faced with the reality of forced assimilation into a culture not their own, a process that, ill economic consequences aside, would surely destroy the fabric of their tribal identity. Worse, the Seminoles were virtually without voice in the process, although they did have friends and supporters both in the legislature and in the local community. The need for a formal tribal organization became apparent to protect Seminole interests (thus cattle owners on the Big Cypress, Hollywood, and Brighton reservations were early supporters of tribal organization), and despite the Seminoles being spared from termination in 1955, momentum carried forward which resulted in the federal recognition of the Seminole Tribe in 1957.

Others were more leery about dealing with the government on any terms and had been cautious over the years in their involvement with government programs. More concerned with maintaining traditional ways of life, termination meant less to them as they were less involved with the government anyway. These Indians tended to live along the Tamiami Trail, and they had over the years developed their own identity as the "Trail Indians" or Trail Miccosukee. Like Cowkeeper had done nearly two hundred years earlier when he held himself apart from the Creek Nation at the Treaty of Picolata near St. Augustine, so too the Trail Miccosukees held out from the Seminole effort to gain federal recognition. When they did seek recognition several years later, it was on their own terms and followed Buffalo Tiger's 1961 trip to Cuba seeking Castro's blessing.

The issue of land claims also divided the Seminoles and Miccosukees. In 1950, a small group of reservation Seminoles with legal backing filed a suit before the Indian Claims Commission, seeking compensation for Florida lands lost through treaties before the Second Seminole War and to Everglades National Park in 1935. The Trail Indians withheld involvement in the suit, correctly perceiving the government intention to forever close the door on future claims. In 1976, after years of legal entanglements and appeals, the Indian Claims Commission awarded the Seminoles approximately $16 million for lands lost prior to the Second Seminole War. Specifically, the money was to be distributed to the descendants of all those Indians who were living in Florida on September 18, 1823, the date of the Treaty of Moultrie Creek. This meant figuring out an equitable means of splitting the money four ways: to the members of the Seminole Nation of Oklahoma, descended from those Florida Seminoles deported to Oklahoma during the Second and Third Seminole wars; to the members of the federally recognized Seminole and Miccosukee tribes of Florida, both descended from those who survived the wars and remained in Florida; and to the Independents, Seminoles who chose not to join either the Seminole or Miccosukee tribes.

Not until 1990 was the distribution problem solved, and this by congressional mandate for a 75/25 split between the Oklahoma and Florida tribes based on population counts. By 1990, the award had grown to $50 million with interest; thus the Florida Seminoles, Miccosukees, and Independents together received about $12.3 million to share. Federal guidelines stipulated that tribal monies were to be divided on a per capita basis and also allocated for economic development. As of 1995, the Miccosukee share (about 18.6 percent) remained undistributed, again reflecting their ambivalence toward governmental mandates and regulations.

Despite the distinct modern political histories of the Seminole and Miccosukee tribes and the fundamental differences between them, attempting to identify any significant historical, cultural, or archaeological differences between the tribes is a difficult task indeed.

The difference is not one of language. The Miccosukees speak the Mikasuki language, as do all but the Brighton Seminoles, who speak Muskogee. Historical accounts describing the different tongues spoken by the Seminoles are of no use except to differentiate the ancestors of the Brighton group from the other Seminoles.

The difference is not one of material culture, at least that portion known through artifacts. Pottery, the favorite domain of archaeologists, provides no certain clues, because all known Seminole pottery found at archaeological sites throughout North and Central Florida shows strong affinity to the Creek pottery tradition, which itself was shared by people speaking several distinct languages. Again, it is the Brighton Seminoles whose separate history might more easily be documented. Over the years, a number of Seminole pottery vessels have been found at locations in the Kissimmee River valley from the vicinity of Orlando south through Okeechobee County, possibly marking the migration route of the Tallahassee (or Tallasay) band of Muskogee-speaking Seminoles south to the Cow Creek area near the present Brighton Reservation.

But can a separate history of the Miccosukee Tribe be developed? Maybe. But maybe it is misguided to look to historical documents of the nineteenth century and the lost artifacts of long ago for evidence. History is, of course, an ongoing process. Current events, after the passage of time, become historical. If the history of the Miccosukee Tribe begins in the Tamiami Trail camps of the 1930s, this in no way diminishes its legitimacy but rather challenges us to better understand the complex factors that stimulate the development of group identity in the recent past.

Seminoles and Archaeologists: Common Ground?

Although some Native Americans look upon archaeologists with disdain and animosity, the Seminole Tribe in recent years has recognized that archaeologists have a useful role to play in tribal heritage studies and in cultural resource management on reservation lands. The Seminoles have made it clear that their relationship with archaeologists can be a positive one if the philosophy and wishes of the tribe are respected. Archaeological studies of important historical locations and excavations of camp and village sites of previous centuries can supplement the tribal history known to the elders and can provide the written documentation necessary to help preserve sites endangered by development.

In 1990, the Seminole Tribe, under the direction of Chairman James Billie, created the Seminole Heritage Survey and in 1992 retained the Archaeological and Historical Conservancy of Miami to conduct a statewide survey and assessment of potential heritage sites. Focusing first on lands near the Big Cypress Reservation, the survey, with funding from the National Park Service, eventually expanded to include a compilation of all recorded Seminole archaeological sites listed in the Florida Site File in Tallahassee.

On reservation lands, the Seminoles have used archaeological surveys to identify archaeological site locations prior to building new homes or bringing new land into citrus agriculture. A major emphasis of such work is to avoid disturbing burial mounds or the final resting places of the Seminole dead. Although the circumstances of disturbing or excavating human skeletal remains are the most problematic for the tribe, we have already seen in the discussion of the Fort Brooke project in Tampa how the discovery and excavation of the Seminole burials from the Seminole War era benefited the Seminoles of the present day.

Whether archaeological knowledge itself will be perceived as having educational value is still an open question. The Seminoles rightly have been little concerned with archaeology for archaeology's sake. The tribe has contributed funding to the archaeological survey and excavation of the Izard battle site, the location on the Withlacoochee River where the Seminoles under Osceola pinned down soldiers led by General Edmund Gaines under heavy fire in March 1836. Although the primary goal of the project was to identify the site for preservation purposes, information was revealed about Seminole strategy and tactics throughout the ten-day siege. The Izard project, although small, can be taken as an indication of Seminole willingness to support archaeological projects beyond their immediate purview, projects that might yield information and knowledge beyond the strict objectives of preservation.

The Native American Graves Protection and Repatriation Act (NAGPRA) and Florida's Unmarked Burial Law have brought the Seminoles and Miccosukees into increasing contact with archaeologists and their concerns, because these laws require consultation with the tribes concerning grave goods, sacred objects, and human remains that exist in museum collections and those that might be unearthed through archaeological excavation. Although the Seminole position is clear regarding their right to control such objects and remains from historic Seminole contexts, policies regarding prehistoric materials seem to be developing on a case-by-case basis and not without a certain amount of public pressure. Through their representation on the Florida Governor's Council on Indian Affairs, the Seminoles and Miccosukees are also able to review museum scripts and exhibit designs concerning issues of appropriateness and cultural sensitivity. To date, the Miccosukees have tended to decline participation in such activities and want little to do with discussions about grave goods and skeletal remains.

If the Seminoles decide to embrace archaeology as another way of knowing about their past, then the future of archaeologists in tribal activities is bright. What role archaeology has to play in the Miccosukee Tribe has yet to be determined and is at present not foreseeable.

Challenges to a New Generation

The Seminoles and Miccosukees are who they are because they have continued to define themselves in different terms than the larger society in which they exist. Core elements of Seminole identity such as the Green Corn Dance and the importance of the clan reflect the tenacious persistence of traditional cultural practices through time. The addition of the medicine bundles to the traditional busk ceremony in the nineteenth century shows that Seminole identity, although fundamentally conservative, also has the capacity for flexibility and innovation. Early in the twentieth century, practices that are now viewed to be quintessentially Seminole, such as patchwork and alligator wrestling, were introduced from the outside and were quickly taken up and used to their advantage. The dual capacity for conservatism and innovation is central to Seminole cultural identity and is the key to their success in the modern world.

Despite the recent economic security provided by bingo, smoke shops, and gaming, daunting challenges to the Seminole and Miccosukee people remain. The leaders among them understand that progress cannot be made at the expense of tribal integrity. Participation in the larger world economy and geopolitics cannot require the sacrifice of cultural values, what it means to be Seminole. To do so would only accelerate what may eventually be inevitable anyway, the total assimilation of the Seminoles into mainstream American society. James Billie was quoted in the June 1, 1986, edition of the *Orlando Sentinel* as saying, "a couple of hundred years from now there won't be any Seminoles. We'll all be intermarried and swallowed up by the white man . . . so all any of us can do is fight as hard as we can to hold onto what little the white man has left of our culture and blood."

The elders have taken up the fight, particularly the aging matriarchs like Ruby Tiger Osceola who are eager to pass down their knowledge of Seminole history and culture to a new generation. It is the challenge of this new generation to learn the new ways and accommodate the old, to keep the Seminole fire burning.

8

On the Seminole Trail

The history of Florida's Seminole and Miccosukee people exists not only in books and dusty drawers of archaeological museums. Their story has a physical dimension as well, the cultural landscape of the Seminole and Miccosukee past as embedded in the geography of modern Florida. Although we can never truly know what it was like to ride with Bartram on his journey across the vast Alachua savanna to Cowkeeper's Cuscowilla in the 1770s, to watch Osceola's Seminoles dance on the banks of the Withlacoochee in 1836, or to witness the frenzy of the ball game at Pine Island Ridge, the past can come alive for us in some small measure by experiencing the landscapes on which these past events occurred.

The Seminoles have made little impact on the Florida landscape, only rarely leaving any permanent or substantial trace of their activities. One can walk the fields that once held their villages and find no clue as to the lives once lived there save for the occasional broken bits of pottery or sherds of glass. For its part, Florida has been quick to reclaim for its own soil trod upon by human feet. But the Seminoles themselves found little need to expend large amounts of labor to alter their surroundings. Their chiefs required no large mounds to stand upon for their pronouncements, nor were gods worshipped there. Burial mounds were not needed for the elite, as there were no elite, at least compared to the societies of late prehistory, and both the dead and living were too few to sustain the practice of mound burial. And the Seminoles did not have to change the earth to make a living from it. Greener pastures could be had by moving to them, more productive fields by finding virgin hammocks.

But the history of the Seminoles and Miccosukees cannot be understood without knowing that geography had an important role in shaping their cultural identity. Indeed, certain areas are so integral to understanding the Seminole past that without knowing what they looked like, the lay of the land, one can only incompletely grasp the events that took place there. The

Alachua savanna (today's Paynes Prairie), the lower Suwannee River, the great Cove of the Withlacoochee, the Big Cypress, the Pine Island Ridge, all were areas sought by the Seminoles as desirable places to live and were ultimately given up by them only under extreme duress.

The reader is encouraged to follow the trail of Seminole history described in this section. By no means a complete listing of important locations, what follows includes sites on public or publicly accessible lands, most of which also include some level of public interpretation. Grouped into four broad geographical areas—the Panhandle, North Florida, Central Florida, and South Florida, the sites reflect the cultural journey of the Seminoles southward through the peninsula.

PANHANDLE: TALLAHASSEE AND POINTS WEST

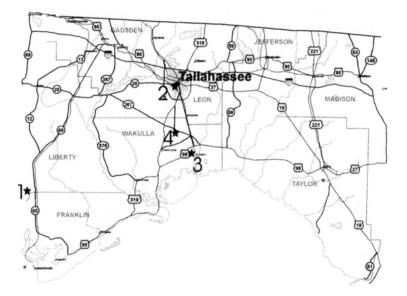

8.1. Seminole sites in the Panhandle.

Negro Fort (Fort Gadsden), Fort Gadsden Historic Site

Historical context: The fort was built in Spanish Florida by the British for use in the War of 1812. When the war ended, British commander Colonel Nicholls left the fort in the possession of free blacks, escaped slaves, and Creek and Seminole Indians. With the fort was left a substantial supply of gunpowder, artillery, and other weapons. As the so-called Negro Fort, the area became a magnet for additional runaway slaves and others wishing to escape American authority. Alarmed at the buildup of potential hostilities so close to U.S. territory, General Andrew Jackson in July 1816 ordered an American supply convoy upriver from Apalachicola Bay past the fort at Prospect Bluff to force a conflict. When four sailors were killed, the fort was surrounded by U.S. troops and called upon to surrender. Following refusal of the blacks and Indians to do so, a bombardment was launched from a nearby gunboat. A "hot shot" exploded the powder magazine, destroying the fort and killing 270 of the more than 300 people inside. Inside the remains of the fort were found ten cannons, 2,500 muskets, 500 carbines, and 500 swords. In 1818 a second fort, Fort Gadsden, was built by Andrew Jackson as a supply base for his raids on Seminole villages in peninsular Florida, despite Florida still being in Spanish hands.

What's there: A short walking trail from the parking area leads to the remains of the fort earthworks. Exhibits in a kiosk at the parking area and picnic grounds interpret the history of the area, display artifacts from the site and vicinity, and present a miniature replica of Fort Gadsden. Brochures are available.

How to get there: Fort Gadsden Historic Site is six miles south of Sumatra and approximately twenty-four miles north of Apalachicola. From U.S. 98 in Green Point, travel north on C.R. 65 toward Sumatra. Watch for signs for park entrance on the left. There is no admission charge.

Map location: 1.

For further information: Contact Apalachicola Ranger District, USDA Forest Service, P.O. Box 579, Highway 20, Bristol, Florida 32321, (904) 643-2282.

Museum of Florida History

R. A. Gray Building, 500 S. Bronough Street, Tallahassee.

Historical context: Exhibits in the Museum of Florida History focus on the period of the Seminole wars, beginning in the early 1800s.

What's there: Artifacts and dioramas emphasize the military aspects of the early U.S. involvement with the Seminoles.

How to get there: The Museum of Florida History is in downtown Tallahassee, several blocks west of the Capitol at Bronough and Pensacola streets. There is paid public parking in a garage at the south end of the building. There is no admission charge.

Map location: 2.

For further information: Open Monday through Friday 9 A.M. to 4:30 P.M., Saturday 10 A.M. to 4:30 P.M., Sunday and holidays noon to 4:30 P.M.. Closed December 25. Call (850) 488-1484.

San Marcos de Apalache

Historical context: An important trading location for the Lower Creeks and early Seminoles during the first Spanish period, the fort continued in use by the English from 1763 to 1783. In 1787, Spain reoccupied the fort but lost it again for a five-week period to William Augustus Bowles and his force of four hundred Creek Indians in 1800. Bowles, self-proclaimed King of Florida and white by birth, had spent years attempting to consolidate power among the Lower Creeks and Seminoles and was an enemy of both Spain and the trading house of Panton, Leslie, and Company, who held much Indian debt. Bowles was eventually captured among the Upper Creeks through English intervention and was returned to Spanish authorities.

In 1818, General Andrew Jackson attacked and captured the fort, still in Spanish Florida, as part of his invasion of the northern part of the peninsula. After capturing and executing two British citizens whom he felt responsible for instigating Indian raids into U.S. territory, Jackson withdrew north, leaving the fort once again to the Spanish. The fort came under official U.S. control in 1821 and was turned over to the territory of Florida in 1824.

What's there: A visitor center contains exhibits on all aspects of the fort's history, and earthworks and other architectural remains of the fort can be seen from a nature trail.

How to get there: San Marcos de Apalache is in Wakulla County on C.R. 363 south of U.S. 98, approximately sixteen miles south of Tallahassee.

Map location: 3.

For further information: Contact San Marcos de Apalache State Historic Site, Box 27, St. Marks, Florida 32355, (850) 925-6216.

Wakulla Springs, Wakulla Springs State Park

Historical context: After the Creek War of 1813–1814, the Creek prophet Hillis Hadjo, or Francis, sought refuge in Spanish Florida, establishing a town on the Wakulla River within, it is believed, the present boundaries of Wakulla Springs State Park. During Jackson's subsequent invasion of

Spanish Florida in 1818, one of his soldiers, Duncan McKrimmon, was captured by the Indians and taken to Francis's Town. Francis's daughter apparently intervened to possibly save McKrimmon's life, and he was taken downstream to San Marcos de Apalache to exchange for ransom. There Francis himself was captured and subsequently hanged by Jackson. An archaeological site identified as 8WA312 is reported to be Francis's Town. Chattahoochee Brushed pottery sherds and glass bottle fragments recovered in an archaeological survey provide some evidence for this identification.

What's there: There is no public interpretation within the park relating to Francis, but the presumed town site can be seen from the river as a clearing a short distance south of the springs. Wakulla Springs itself is a major public attraction and can be viewed from a glass-bottom boat or on a river cruise.

How to get there: Wakulla Springs State Park is approximately sixteen miles south of Tallahassee. It can be reached by following signs on S.R. 61 south of its intersection with S.R. 267.

Map location: 4.

For further information: Contact Wakulla Springs State Park, 1 Spring Drive, Wakulla Springs, Florida 32305, (850) 922-3632. The Wakulla Springs Lodge can be reached by calling (850) 224-5950.

North Florida: Tallahassee to Bushnell

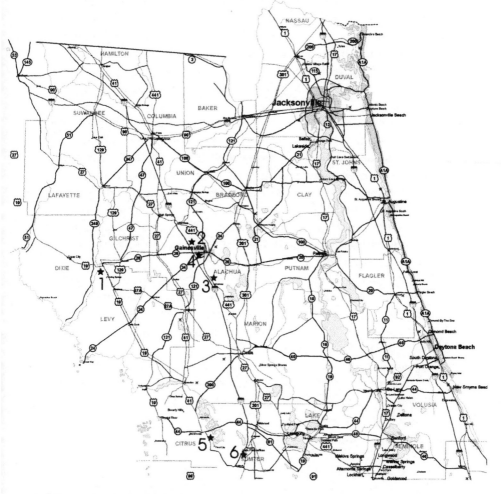

8.2. Seminole sites in North Florida.

Suwannee River at Fanning Springs Bridge

Historical context: Just after crossing the Suwannee River bridge, U.S. 19 runs parallel to the river for approximately one mile. This was the location of Bowlegs' Town and an associated village of Black Seminoles in 1818 during Andrew Jackson's offensive against the Seminoles. The best primary account of this invasion, complete with a map, is that of Hugh Young, published in the *Florida Historical Quarterly* in 1934–1935. Well prior to

Bowlegs, this western portion of the bend was occupied by Seminoles of the White King's village in the 1760s prior to their relocation to Talahasochte on the east bank in the 1770s. John Goggin's underwater recovery of Seminole artifacts from the Oven Hill site and the more limited finds in the terrestrial portion of the site may relate to this early occupation.

This portion of the Suwannee River from the Fanning Springs vicinity south to Manatee Springs saw heavy Seminole use. The town of Talahasochte visited by William Bartram was located on the east bank of the river in the vicinity of Manatee Springs State Park. It was at Manatee Springs itself that Bartram observed the manatee remains butchered by the Seminoles the previous winter. Bartram devoted much detailed description to Talahasochte and its natural surroundings on the Suwannee River. Mentions of the 1760s village on the west bank can be found in the journal of Denys Rolle, republished by the University of Florida Press in 1977.

What's there: There is no public interpretation in the area pertaining to the Seminoles, but one who goes armed with a copy of Bartram's *Travels* will have little difficulty imagining the scene.

How to get there: A highway rest stop on the south side of U.S. 19 east of the Suwannee River bridge allows parking and a view of the river. The river can be reached by descending a set of steps at the parking lot. Manatee Springs State Park can be reached by turning west on S.R. 320 (Manatee Springs Road) from U.S. 19 north of Chiefland.

Map location: 1.

For further information: Contact Manatee Springs State Park, 11650 N.W. 115th Street, Chiefland, Florida 32626, (352) 493-4288.

San Felasco Hammock

Managed by Devil's Millhopper State Geological Site

Historical context: The former location of the Timucua mission San Francisco de Potano (San Francisco becoming San Felasco in the Indian pronunciation), this vast hammock was home to a small band of Seminoles in 1824 whose leader was also a blacksmith. James Pierce attended an "annual feast" here and published his observations in 1825, noting that both men and women danced around a central dance track, the men with their faces painted with catlike whiskers. On September 18, 1836, during the Second Seminole War, the Seminoles here attacked a militia unit commanded by Colonel John Warren, who would two months later see action again in the Battle of the Wahoo Swamp.

What's there: There is no public interpretation of the former Seminole occupation, but hiking trails allow access to the preserve.

How to get there: On C.R. 232 (N.W. 63rd Blvd.) about four miles west of entrance to the Devil's Millhopper State Geological Site in northwest Gainesville. Trails lead from public parking on the south side of the road.

Map location: 2.

For further information: Contact Devil's Millhopper State Geological Site, 4732 N.W. Millhopper Road, Gainesville, Florida, (352) 955-2008.

Paynes Prairie, Paynes Prairie State Preserve

Historical context: Without question one of the most important areas in the development of Seminole culture, it was here that Cowkeeper's original band of Oconee Creeks settled in the 1760s, first at a village on the rim of the Alachua savanna and then at Cuscowilla, a few miles south. Bartram's several visits to the prairie provide our best early glimpse of Seminole life.

Seminole archaeological sites have been identified on the north side of the prairie (site 8AL296, reported by William Sears), on the east side (Goggin's Zetrouer site burials near Rochelle), and in the southern portion of the preserve (the location of King Payne's house site), but surprisingly, the major town of Cuscowilla remains archaeologically undetected.

After Cowkeeper's death, leadership of the Alachua band passed to his nephew, known as King Payne. Payne's Seminoles were attacked by Georgia militia led by Colonel Daniel Newnan in 1811, resulting in a brief pitched battle that took place between the present settlement of Rochelle and the southeast margin of Newnans Lake. Payne later died of wounds sustained in the fighting and was eventually succeeded by his nephew Micanopy. Soon after Payne's death, the Alachua Seminoles were again under attack, this time by combined Georgia and Tennessee militia aimed at the town of Bowlegs, Payne's brother. This village was located several miles southwest of the present town of Micanopy in the hammock margin of a small prairie. Bowlegs moved west to the Suwannee River, Micanopy south to Okahumpka on the banks of Lake Harris south of Leesburg.

Although never again the center of Seminole occupation, the Paynes Prairie area continued to figure importantly in historical events leading to the Second Seminole War. One such event was the so-called Battle of Black Point, an attack on a supply train led by Osceola on December 18, 1835.

What's there: A visitor center on the edge of the prairie includes exhibits on Bartram and Seminole history, supplemented by artifacts. The nearby observation tower offers a sweeping view of the basin itself. A short trail from a parking area on the north side of the rim, accessible from S.E. 15th Street, crosses the area of the former Spanish cattle ranch and leads to the Alachua Sink. North of the prairie, on the west side of C.R. 234 a short distance north of its intersection with S.R. 20 (Hawthorne Road), once stood a bronze plaque erected by the United Daughters of the Confederacy marking the general location of the battle between Daniel Newnan and Payne on the east side of Newnans Lake. The plaque is now gone, but the concrete base remains. Historical markers at the U.S. 441 Observation Platform on the prairie and in the town of Micanopy, southwest of the prairie, describe Bartram's travels through the area.

How to get there: The main entrance to Paynes Prairie State Preserve is located ten miles south of Gainesville and one mile north of Micanopy on U.S. 441. The Bolen Bluff Trail, the U.S. 441 Observation Platform, and the North Rim/Alachua Sink trail can be accessed by following road signs.

Map location: 3.

For further information: Paynes Prairie State Preserve, Route 2, Box 41, Micanopy, Florida, (352) 466-3397.

8.3. Paynes Prairie as it appears today. (Courtesy of the Florida Park Service, Department of Environmental Protection.)

8.4. The Visitor Center, Paynes Prairie State Preserve, highlights Seminole history in the area. (Photograph courtesy of the Florida Park Service, Department of Environmental Protection.)

Florida Museum of Natural History

Historical context: Formerly known as the Florida State Museum, this facility, billed as the largest natural history museum in the southeastern United States, has long been the major repository of Florida's aboriginal artifacts and contains many important archaeological research collections representing all culture periods. Collections from the early Florida Park Service archaeological survey program directed by John Griffin and materials from the Department of Anthropology at the University of Florida largely obtained by John Goggin are curated here.

What's there: The Research Collections hold Seminole artifacts from Goggin's excavations at Oven Hill in the Suwannee River, from the burials near Paynes Prairie, from Spalding's Lower Store, a trading house on the St. Johns River, and from Sears's excavations at 8AL296, among others. Cultural materials include a beaded shoulder pouch and buckskin clothing obtained from a dead warrior in 1857 in the Big Cypress area and John Goggin's collection of Seminole silverwork, mostly dating from the 1940s. Access to the research collections is by appointment only.

The Hall of South Florida People and Environments in Powell Hall will exhibit artifacts relating to the Seminole and Miccosukee peoples and interpret their cultural adaptations to the region.

How to get there: The research and collections building, J. C. Dickinson Hall, is located on the corner of Newell Drive and Museum Road on the University of Florida campus. Powell Hall, the exhibit facility, is located between the Samuel P. Harn Museum of Art and the Performing Arts Center, on the west side of the campus, accessible from S.W. 34th Street.

Map location: 4.

For further information: Contact the Florida Museum of Natural History, (352) 392-1721 (Research and Collections) or (352) 846-2000 (Powell Hall). *Web address:* http://www.flmnh.ufl.edu/admin/intro.htm#Top

Cove of the Withlacoochee

Withlacoochee River–Lake Tsala Apopka vicinity from S.R. 200 south to S.R. 48, Inverness area of eastern Citrus County, also portions of Sumter and Marion counties.

Historical context: The so-called Cove of the Withlacoochee is a one-hundred-square mile wetland formed in the bend of the Withlacoochee River where it meanders north around the Lake Tsala Apopka chain east of Inverness in Citrus County. This was a heartland area of Seminole villages in the early years of the American presence in Florida and was repeatedly targeted by military offensives in the first years of the Second Seminole War. Arguably some of the most dramatic episodes in the clash between the United States and the Seminole took place in the Cove, from the unsuccessful attempts by both General Clinch and General Gaines to penetrate the Seminole stronghold between December 31, 1835, and early March 1836 to the scorched-earth sweeps of later that year. It was here that the coordinated attack on Wiley Thompson at Fort King and Dade's command advancing on the Fort King Road was planned by Osceola, Jumper, Alligator, and Micanopy, and it was here, deep in the swamps, that Osceola's wartime refuge, known as "Powell's Town," was located. The Seminoles were eventually driven from the Cove, but the army remained wary of Seminole attempts to reoccupy the region through 1842 and periodically made reconnaissances of the Cove until the end of the war.

What's there: Fort Cooper State Park marks the location of a temporary log palisade quickly erected by Major Mark Anthony Cooper's Georgia volunteers in April 1836 during their push through the Cove under General Winfield Scott's direction. The fort fell under heavy fire several times from Seminole warriors during a two-week siege. A short trail leads from the parking area to the fort location and partial reconstruction based on archaeological excavations. Signs at the site interpret the historical events.

The location of Fort Izard, the temporary log breastwork thrown up by troops under the command of General Gaines under heavy attack by the Seminoles from February 29 through March 10, 1836, is owned by the Southwest Florida Water Management District. No standing remains exist, but the area can be accessed (with prior notification) on a hiking trail. The

Seminole Wars Historic Foundation occasionally conducts guided tours of the site (see contact information at the end of this chapter).

The running battle between a combined force of regulars, militia, and Creek volunteers and the Seminoles on November 21, 1836, on the edge of the Wahoo Swamp is commemorated by a historical marker on S.R. 48 west of the small town of Wahoo. This small roadside park also includes an interpretive kiosk on the expedition of the Spanish conquistador Hernando de Soto in 1539.

For those car-bound and in a hurry, views of the Withlacoochee Cove can be had from a county boat ramp on C.R. 39 north of S.R. 200 (this is the general vicinity of the Seminole force during the Izard battle) and from a roadside park on the Sumter County (east) side of the river at the S.R. 44 crossing.

The Museum of Citrus County History in the Old Courthouse in Inverness contains artifacts of the prehistoric and Seminole cultures of the area.

How to get there: Fort Cooper State Park is located on the Old Floral City Road between Inverness and Floral City, east of U.S. 41, and is clearly marked with state park signs. The Wahoo battle marker is on the north side of S.R. 48 east of Floral City and west of Wahoo. Road signs for the de Soto Trail indicate the location. The Museum of Citrus County History is located in the Old Courthouse in downtown Inverness on U.S. 41.

Map location: 5.

8.5. Reconstructed log palisade at Fort Cooper State Park.

8.6. Seminole pottery vessel found in the Cove of the Withlacoochee. Private collection.

For further information: Fort Cooper State Park, 3100 Old Floral City Road, Inverness, Florida 34450, (352) 726-0315. For the Camp Izard site, contact the Southwest Florida Water Management District or the Seminole Wars Historic Foundation (352) 583-2974, for special events. The Old Courthouse Museum in Inverness can be reached by calling (352) 637-9925, Monday through Friday, 10 A.M. to 2 P.M. For additional information, contact the Citrus County Historical Resources Office, (352) 637-9929.

Dade Battlefield State Historic Site

Historical context: Here on the chilly morning of December 28, 1835, Major Francis Dade and 107 of his men fell under an Indian ambush, fired on by the Seminoles and their black allies concealed behind pine trees and palmettos. Two survivors, both critically wounded, eventually made their way back to Fort Brooke. The Indian attack had been planned by Osceola, Jumper, and Alligator as a two-pronged strike at the threatening U.S. military presence, the other strike occurring later that same day against Indian agent Wiley Thompson at Fort King. The Dade and Thompson attacks and the stiff resistance rallied by the Seminoles against the attempted invasion of the Cove of the Withlacoochee on December 31 by Colonel Duncan Clinch sent a clear message to the United States that the Seminoles would not be removed from Florida without a fight. When the horrid scene of the Dade ambush was finally discovered several months later, the specific locations where Dade and his men had fallen were noted along with the position of the two-sided log breastwork that had been hastily thrown up for the soldiers' last stand.

What's there: A visitor center contains artifacts and exhibits pertaining to the battle. A short walking trail features a reconstruction of the log barricade and monuments to Dade and several of his officers in the locations where they fell. A reenactment of the battle takes place annually on the first weekend of January, in which both reenactors and members of the Seminole Tribe participate. This has become a popular and highly publicized event in recent years and requires early arrival for best parking and best viewing position.

How to get there: The Dade Battlefield State Historic Site is located south of C.R. 476 (Seminole Avenue), west of U.S. 301, east of I-75, and southwest of Bushnell. Access from I-75 is clearly marked; take the Bushnell exit and follow S.R. 48 east, watching for signs.

Map location: 6.

For further information: Contact Dade Battlefield State Historic Site, 7200 C.R. 603, Bushnell, Florida 33513, (352) 793-4781.

CENTRAL FLORIDA: BUSHNELL TO SEBRING

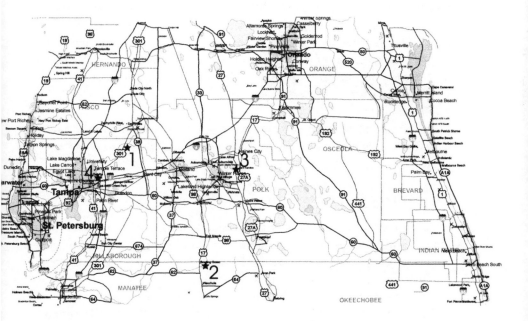

8.7. Seminole sites in Central Florida.

Fort Foster Historic Site

Historical context: Fort Foster was constructed in November and December 1836 to guard the bridge crossing the Hillsborough River on the strategic Fort King Road. A previous fort, Fort Alabama, had been built for this purpose by the Alabama volunteers but had been abandoned in April after two months' occupation. By April 1837, the post took on the task of ensuring that Seminoles arriving to emigrate at Fort Brooke stayed south of the Hillsborough River, while all new white settlers stayed north. When the mass emigration of the Seminoles did not come to pass, interest in maintaining personnel at the fort diminished. Fort Foster was abandoned in the late spring of 1838, its purpose served, and was only briefly reactivated in 1849 when tensions with the Seminoles again flared.

What's there: An authentic reconstruction of the fort, based on archaeological and documentary evidence, is open to the public for ranger-guided tours. For special tours and the annual Fort Foster Day, reenactors re-create military life in the fort. Exhibits and displays in a small visitor center in Hillsborough River State Park contain artifacts from the site and interpretations of the period.

How to get there: Fort Foster is located on the east side of U.S. 301, a short distance north of the entrance to Hillsborough River State Park (which is on the west side of the highway), just south of the Hillsborough River. A loop trail leads from the parking area to the fort. The interpretive center is located on the west side of U.S. 301 across from the fort parking lot. Access to the fort is by admission to Hillsborough River State Park, entrance clearly marked on the west side of U.S. 301.

Map location: 1.

For further information: For tour times and fees, contact Hillsborough River State Park, 15402 U.S. 301 N., Thonotosassa, Florida 33592, (813) 987-6771.

Paynes Creek State Historic Site

Historical context: At the close of the Second Seminole War in 1842, fewer than five hundred Seminoles remained in Florida, protected by the vastness and isolation of the Big Cypress Swamp. As these Seminoles began to establish cautious trade relations with stores on the gulf coast, they came into increasing contact with the white settlers who had moved in to what had formerly been Indian lands. In 1849, the U.S. government allowed the establishment of the Kennedy and Darling store near Paynes Creek in the hope of keeping the Indians restricted to the interior.

A grievance between a small group of Seminoles and the traders escalated into violence. On July 17, 1849, four Seminoles opened fire on three clerks as they sat down to dinner. Two of the clerks, Captain George S. Payne and Dempsey Whiddon, were killed, and the store was burned. Bowlegs, wanting to avoid open conflict, ordered the men captured. Three were caught and turned over to authorities, the fourth was killed by the Seminoles. Nonetheless, the government prepared for renewed warfare, establishing a new chain of forts, while reactivating others, such as Fort Foster on the Hillsborough.

Construction began on Fort Chokonikla on October 26, 1849, a short distance north of the former Kennedy and Darling store. Sickness and disease rather than Indian bullets took their toll on the unfortunate soldiers stationed there, and the post was abandoned in July 1850.

What's there: A visitor center contains exhibits on the Seminoles, events at the trading post, and Fort Chokonikla. Hiking trails lead from the visitor center to the fort site and from the parking lot to the grave site of George Payne and Dempsey Whiddon and to the area of the store.

How to get there: Paynes Creek State Historic Site is located in Hardee County east of Bowling Green. Go east from U.S. 17 on C.R. 664-A (Lake Branch Road), following signs to the park.

Map location: 2.

For further information: Paynes Creek State Historic Site, P.O. Box 547, Bowling Green, Florida 33834, (941) 375-4717.

Chipco Commemorative Plaque, Lake Hamilton

Historical context: Before moving to Catfish Creek and Lake Pierce in the 1880s, Chipco of the Tallahassee band lived on Bonar Island in Lake Hamilton. An account of 1890 tells of the island's new landowner finding a Seminole log mortar and dugout canoe at the abandoned village site. Chipco, who is said to have told of once killing a white child, became a friend of whites in his later years. This marker commemorates that friendship.

What's there: A simple concrete marker with a plaque bears this inscription: "In Memory of Chipco, Lover of Peace, friend of the White Man. His Seminole Indian Village was Located on Bonar's Island in Lake Hamilton 1855. Dedicated by the Ponce De Leon Chapter, Daughters of the American Revolution, Winter Haven, Florida, 1957."

How to get there: The marker is located in a small roadside park on the west side of U.S. 27 on the south side of Lake Hamilton. A view of Bonar Island is possible from the parking area.

8.8. The Chipco plaque on U.S. 27 near Lake Hamilton.

Map location: 3.

For further information: None should be required. For a more detailed account of Chipco and the Tallahassees, see chapter 4.

Tampa Reservation, Seminole Tribe of Florida

Historical context: Established in 1981 as a location to rebury the Seminole skeletal remains unearthed from the Fort Brooke cemetery prior to the construction of the municipal parking garage, the reservation quickly grew to include a bingo hall, smoke shop, and hotel complex.

What's there: "Bobby Henry's Seminole Indian Village, Gift Shop, and Museum" are on the grounds. Artifacts from the Fort Brooke burials are on display, and the skeletal remains from the site have been reinterred within. There is an admission fee for the museum.

How to get there: The reservation is located at 5221 Orient Road and is visible from I-4 west of the U.S. 301 interchange. From 301, travel west on Hillsborough, turn left (south) on Orient Road, or west on Martin Luther King Blvd. and north (right) on Orient Road over I-4. Or take exit 5 off I-4 and drive north one-quarter of a mile.

Map location: 4.

For further information: Call (813) 620-3077.

South Florida: Sebring South

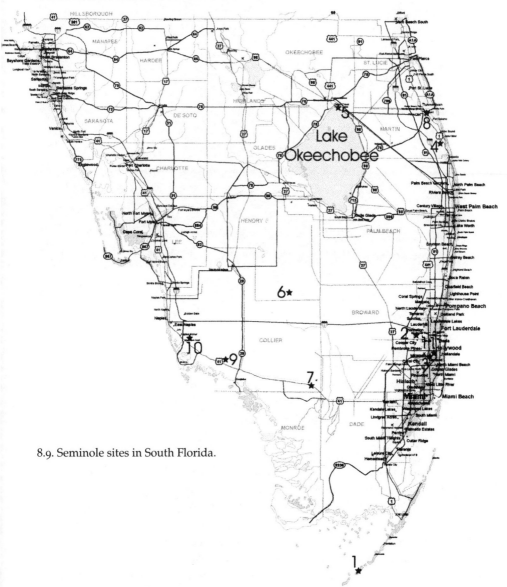

8.9. Seminole sites in South Florida.

Indian Key State Historic Site

Historical context: It was here on August 7, 1840, that the infamous Chakaika led the attack on the small port settlement, killing the noted botanist Henry Perrine. Perrine had sought the island's seclusion for his horticultural experiments during the Second Seminole War. All but one of the town's build-

8.10. Indian Key, in the Atlantic Ocean east of U.S. 1, near Lower Matecumbe Key. Clearing in center is area of town square. (Photograph courtesy of the Florida Park Service, Department of Environmental Protection.)

ings were destroyed in the attack and the plunder hauled off to Chakaika's hideaway in the Everglades.

The town of Indian Key was founded in 1831 by Jacob Housman as a center for wreck salvaging in the upper Keys. In 1836, Indian Key became the county seat for newly established Dade County. The island was only sparsely reinhabited after the Chakaika raid and was abandoned in the early part of the twentieth century.

What's there: An observation tower provides a view of the island; trails follow the original streets through the ruins of the town, which include a town square, hotel, warehouse, cisterns, and the grave of Jacob Housman.

How to get there: Indian Key is accessible only by boat. The Florida Park Service offers three-hour boat tours from Indian Key Fill on U.S. 1. There is a fee, and reservations are recommended. Indian Key is in the Indian Key Channel between Upper Matecumbe Key and Lower Matecumbe Key.

Map location: 1.

For further information: Contact Indian Key State Historic Site, P.O. Box 1052, Islamorada, Florida 33036, (305) 664-4815.

Pine Island Ridge

Historical context: The Pine Island Ridge complex was the core area of Seminole settlement in the eastern Everglades, settled by the 1830s and perhaps earlier. Larger villages were more possible here than elsewhere in the Everglades, and this form of social organization, consisting of people joined together through extended kin relationships, persisted through the end of the nineteenth century. Historian Patsy West reports that up to 40 percent of today's Seminole and Miccosukee tribes as well as the Independents are descended from Pine Island families, particularly those of the nearby Dania Reservation. The ridge was also the center of busk or Green Corn ceremonies for South Florida groups. Rare photographs of an 1897 ball game at the dance ground provide a privileged glimpse of this aspect of Seminole culture.

Pine Island Ridge was targeted by the military during the Second Seminole War. One attack resulted in a skirmish fought on the northern portion of the ridge in 1838. However, Seminole occupation on Pine Island seemed to be on the increase in the latter half of the century. Encroachments from an expanding white presence in South Florida led to the abandonment of the Pine Island camps early in the twentieth century, with only a small portion of land legally set aside for the Dania Reservation.

Intensive efforts mounted by local preservation groups, Broward County, and the town of Davie and supported by the Seminole Tribe resulted in the purchase of nearly one hundred acres of the southern arm of the ridge using $3.56 million of the State of Florida's Conservation and Recreation Lands (CARL) acquisition funds in the early 1990s. An adjacent parcel containing archaeological evidence of Seminole occupation has been preserved as green space by the town of Davie.

What's there: Exhibit panels in the visitor center depict the life of Abiaka (Sam Jones) and the Battle of Pine Island Ridge. Outside the visitor center is a bronze sculpture of Abiaka pointing a woman and child to safety. This sculpture, commissioned by Broward County, was dedicated in 1995. Hiking trails lead across the ridge and are accessible through Tree Tops Park, managed by the Broward County Parks and Recreation Department. There are eleven recorded archaeological sites on the grounds, most of which date to the prehistoric Glades periods. These sites are not specifically marked. The dance ground and village shown in the 1897 photographs probably are on the parcel managed by the town of Davie.

How to get there: Tree Tops Park is reached from Pine Island Road between I-595 and Orange Drive. Entrance is from S.W. 100th Avenue.

8.11. Sculpture of Sam Jones pointing the way to safety, Tree Tops Park trailhead to the Pine Island Ridge.

Map location: 2.

For further information: Contact Broward County Parks and Recreation Department, Tree Tops Park, (954) 370-3750. An admission fee is charged.

Snake Warriors Island

Historical context: During the Second Seminole War in 1841, William Harney's invading troops found two abandoned Seminole towns, their dance grounds, a council lodge, and agricultural fields (including a patch of Cuban tobacco). Left behind by the Snake Warrior (Chitto Tustenuggee) and his Seminoles were such items as war dance masks, baskets, kettles, and fish spears. The Seminoles may have been at this location as early as 1828 when the Snake Creek area was visited by John Lee Williams. At that time Williams noted that Snake Warrior had only recently arrived and that sixty Seminoles from Sam Jones's village had just resettled there. Williams observed that twenty acres had been cleared and two villages constructed. These may be the same two noted in 1841. Chitto Tustenuggee himself may have been a Creek who came to Florida after the Creek War of 1814. Clearly by the period of the Second Seminole War he had become allied with Sam Jones. Chitto Tustenuggee died in March 1852.

As was the case with Pine Island Ridge, by 1870 Snake Warriors Island and the Snake Creek area became a nucleus of Seminole settlement, led by Old Alec and Old Tiger Tail. Tiger Tail's Seminoles had increasing contact with white society and were frequently seen traveling to trading houses on the Miami River. Inevitably, however, conflicts with the whites arose, as their numbers too increased. Government survey crews were turned away at the point of a gun, and at least one "Indian Scare" panicked local residents. As the century came to a close, expanding development finally overwhelmed the Snake Creek camps, and they were abandoned. Some of the Seminoles went to Pine Island Ridge, others dispersed further into the interior.

The site was saved from a developer's bulldozer through the cooperative efforts of the Trust for Public Lands, the Resolution Trust Corporation, Broward County, the Archaeological and Historical Conservancy, the Seminole Tribe, and the State of Florida. Fifty-three acres were purchased in 1992 using nearly $2 million of the state's Emergency Archaeological Acquisition Fund. Remains of the Seminole occupation have been discovered in archaeological surveys of the tract. Artifacts found include projectile points made from sheet copper and sheet brass, military buttons, glass beads, and cast iron kettle fragments.

What's there: Broward County manages the property and plans to use it as a county park. Interpretive plans are under development.

How to get there: Snake Warriors Island is located in Miramar, Broward County, south of S.W. 63rd Street between S.W. 62nd Avenue and S.W. 64th Avenue.

Map location: 3.

For further information: Contact Broward County Parks and Recreation Division, (954) 357-8100.

Battle of the Loxahatchee

Historical context: On January 24, 1838, the advancing army under General Jesup's command encountered a force of several hundred Seminoles drawn up ready for a fight in a hammock beyond a cypress slough near the Loxahatchee River. Spurred on by Jesup's challenge to follow him into battle, the soldiers eventually dislodged the Seminoles from the hammock, at a loss of seven killed and thirty-one wounded, including Jesup himself. Feeling that the Seminole resistance was broken and their culture in shambles, Jesup urged an end to the war and recommended to the secretary of war that the Seminoles remaining in Florida be left alone in the wilderness. His request denied, Jesup resorted to his earlier practice of capturing the Indians by any subterfuge necessary. By April 1838, Jesup had been relieved of command, at his own request. The most successful Indian fighter of the Seminole War, Jesup was responsible for the capture of some 2,900 Seminoles and the death of one hundred others in combat.

The Seminoles took a stand at Loxahatchee to protect a nearby village from discovery and attack. Settlement in this area almost certainly dispersed after Jesup's assault. The Loxahatchee area was later resettled by small bands of Seminoles. Remains of one such camp may have been discovered in an archaeological survey of Palm Beach County's Riverbend Park, where glass trade beads, a rum bottle, engineer's calipers, and musket balls were found.

What's there: Portions of the battle are thought to have been fought in Jonathan Dickinson State Park on the banks of the Loxahatchee River, with the rest of the engagement having taken place on state-controlled land on the other side. A sign in Jonathan Dickinson State Park interprets the battle.

How to get there: Jonathan Dickinson State Park is located at 16450 S.E. Federal Highway (U.S. 1) in Hobe Sound.

Map location: 4.

For further information: Contact Jonathan Dickinson State Park, 16450 S.E. Federal Highway, Hobe Sound, Florida 33455, (407) 744-9814.

Battle of Okeechobee

Historical context: On the morning of Christmas Day 1837, more than 1,000 troops commanded by Colonel Zachary Taylor moved across an open prairie on the north shore of Lake Okeechobee to face several hundred Seminole warriors led by Sam Jones, Alligator, and Wildcat in what would be the only major pitched fight of the Second Seminole War. Less than three hours later, twenty-seven soldiers lay dead, another 111 wounded, but the Indian front had been broken. One month later when army units returned to survey the battlefield, the remains of eleven Indian dead were discovered, but the warriors had long since dispersed to the Big Cypress Swamp or in the direction of Pine Island Ridge in the eastern Everglades. The Second Seminole War lasted another five years, but the Seminoles were never again able to amass a fighting force capable of direct confrontation with the military. On the U.S. side, the heavy losses resulting from this pitched battle, among the heaviest ever sustained in the Indian wars, were a clear indication of the high price of victory.

Although the Okeechobee battle was the culmination of General Thomas Jesup's four-prong offensive against the South Florida Seminoles, the glory went to Taylor, the only American leader to emerge from the war with an enhanced reputation. Taylor rode to national fame as "Old Rough and Ready" in the Mexican War and was elected to the presidency in 1848. Jesup spent the rest of his career defending his actions as commander, which included seizing Osceola, Micanopy, and other prominent Seminoles under flags of truce.

What's there: The general battlefield location is marked by a monument erected in 1939 by the Florida Society of the Daughters of the American Revolution. Archaeological surveys conducted by the Archaeological and Historical Conservancy have resulted in the identification of Taylor's camp, used by the troops before and after the battle, and more precise recording of the battlefield boundaries. Interested readers should consult an article published on this subject by Robert S. Carr, Marilyn Masson, and Willard Steele in *Florida Anthropologist*, September 1989.

How to get there: The battlefield is between U.S. 441 and S.R. 710 on the east side of Taylor Creek about four miles south of the town of Okeechobee. The historical marker is on the north right-of-way of U.S. 441.

Map location: 5.

For further information: See the article by Carr, Masson, and Steele referred to above.

Ah-Tah-Thi-Ki Museum, Big Cypress Seminole Reservation

Historical context: Although the Tampa and Hollywood reservations have small museums, the Ah-Tah-Thi-Ki ("a place to remember") Museum is the first true tribal museum. After nearly thirty years of effort and planning, mostly spearheaded by Tribal Chairman James Billie, this $2 million state-of-the-art facility opened in August 1997. There could be no better place for the Seminole museum than the Big Cypress, in many ways the spiritual and cultural core of the Seminole Tribe.

What's there: Artifacts on loan from museums across the country, most notably from the Heye collection of the Smithsonian's National Museum of the American Indian, supported by photographic images copied from Patsy West's monumental archival collection, tell the story of Seminole culture and history, from the Seminole wars to hunting, fishing, and camp life, to the Green Corn Dance. Interactive videos and films on Seminole culture and language broaden the museum's appeal to people accustomed to multimedia entertainment.

How to get there: The Ah-Tah-Thi-Ki Museum is located on the Big Cypress Reservation. Signs from Exit 14 on I-75 (Alligator Alley) direct the visitor to the museum, which is about seventeen miles north of the exit.

Map location: 6.

For further information: The museum is open Tuesday through Sunday. There is an admission fee. Call (954) 792-0745 for specific information. Its web address is http://www.seminoletribe.com/museum.

Miccosukee Reservation, Forty-Mile Bend
(Miccosukee Tribe of Indians)

Historical context: The Miccosukee Tribe of Indians of Florida received federal recognition in 1962, thus establishing a political identity separate from the Seminole Tribe. Many of the early tribal members lived in family camps along the Tamiami Trail where they combined a tourist economy with the pursuit of traditional hunting, fishing, and gathering lifeways in the Everglades. Today the Miccosukees pride themselves on their ability to keep traditional spiritual and medicine knowledge alive.

What's there: The Miccosukee Indian Village contains chickees, craft demonstrations, and a museum in which Miccosukee culture and history are interpreted. The visitor is also encouraged to drive through the reservation where modern housing, tribal schools, a health clinic, and other administrative offices can be seen. Approximately one-quarter of a mile east

8.12. Miccosukee Reservation on the Tamiami Trail, 1998.

of the Indian Village is the Miccosukee Restaurant and the Information Center. Other attractions include airboat rides to a hammock camp in the Everglades. There is a fee for admission to the Miccosukee Indian Village.

How to get there: The Miccosukee Reservation is located at Forty-Mile Bend on the Tamiami Trail, approximately twenty-five miles west of Miami.

Map location: 7.

For further information: Contact the Miccosukee Tribe of Indians of Florida, P.O. Box 440021, Tamiami Station, Miami, Florida 33144, (305) 223-8380.

Elliot Museum, Willoughby Seminole Collection

Historical context: In 1896–1897 naturalist Hugh C. Willoughby traveled across the Everglades, collecting natural history specimens and bartering with the Seminoles for sofkee spoons and other objects of material culture. His 1898 publication *Across the Everglades* chronicles these trips and describes the Seminoles he encountered.

The museum was founded in 1960 and features the inventions of Sterling Elliot.

What's there: Seminole men's, women's, and children's clothing, ball sticks, turtle shell rattles, and other Seminole objects collected by Willoughby are on display. The museum also houses the Willoughby archives, which is open to researchers by appointment.

How to get there: The Elliot Museum is located on Hutchinson Island's East Ocean Boulevard near Stuart and is open daily from 10:00 A.M. to 4 P.M.

Map location: 8.

For further information: Contact the Elliot Museum, 825 N.E. Ocean Blvd., Hutchinson Island, Stuart, Florida 34996, (561) 225-1961.

Tamiami Trail Villages

Historical context: The opening of the Tamiami Trail in 1928 attracted Seminoles from the lower Big Cypress and western Everglades to resettle at roadside villages. The gas stations placed at regular intervals along the highway provided logical places for the Seminoles to settle and sell beadwork, dolls, patchwork, and other crafts to tourists. By 1939, thirteen established trail villages were documented. The Tamiami Trail villages were not tourist camps, and today the residential areas are not open to the public.

8.13. Indian Village at Weavers Station, Tamiami Trail, 1998.

What's there: Roadside villages exist at Royal Palm Hammock, Weavers Station, Monroe Station, in the vicinity of the Fifty-Mile Bend, and several other locations. Signs posted on the outside of the compounds indicate whether the gift shops are open or closed. Small parking areas allow safe access to the gift shops.

How to get there: Locations are clearly marked on the Tamiami Trail (U.S. 41) by green "Indian Village" signs. The villages at Royal Palm Hammock, Weavers Station, and Monroe Station are particularly well marked and easy to access.

Map locations: 9, 10.

For further information: None should be required.

FOR FURTHER INFORMATION

Florida Anthropological Society

The Florida Anthropological Society (P.O. Box 82255, Tampa, Florida 33682), founded in 1947, has long promoted Seminole Indian studies in the pages of its quarterly journal the *Florida Anthropologist*. Important research by William Sturtevant, Louis Capron, Wilfred Neill, and other scholars first appeared in the journal. Members receive the journal and a quarterly newsletter.

Archaeological and Historical Conservancy

The AHC (P.O. Box 450283, Miami, Florida 33145, [305] 325-0789) has been active and influential in the preservation of important Seminole heritage sites in South Florida, including Pine Island Ridge, Snake Warriors Island, and the Okeechobee battlefield and has also conducted several archaeological surveys of reservation lands for the Seminole Tribe. Members receive the quarterly newsletter *Florida Antiquity*.

The Seminole Wars Historic Foundation, Inc.

Through the efforts of the foundation (35247 Reynolds Avenue, Dade City, Florida 33523, [352] 583-2974), the site of the Second Seminole War Izard battle on the banks of the Withlacoochee River has been preserved. Other preservation projects include support for the protection of the Fort King site and the Fort Dade site. The foundation also supported the publication of the diary of Lieutenant Henry Prince, which contains many firsthand observations of the Seminoles during the Second Seminole War. Members receive a newsletter and invitations to special events.

FURTHER READING

The best single source on Florida Seminole history and culture is William Sturtevant's edited volume *A Seminole Sourcebook*, issued in 1987 by Garland Publishing. This comprehensive compilation of primary references contains classic archaeological studies by John Goggin and Charles Fairbanks, Sturtevant's own ethnohistorical study "Creek into Seminole," first published in 1971, works by Sturtevant and Louis Capron on Seminole medicine bundles and the Green Corn Dance, early twentieth-century travelers' accounts, government reports by Roy Nash and Gene Sterling, and Alexander Spoehr's anthropological study of Seminole clans. William Sturtevant's 1954 doctoral dissertation from Yale University, "The Mikasuki Seminole: Medical Beliefs and Practices" (published in 1979 by University Microfilms) is an important anthropological synthesis of language, history, material culture, ethnology, and oral history. The serious student of Seminole culture will want to read the many other publications of William Sturtevant, the preeminent scholar in Seminole studies.

Two firsthand accounts published slightly more than one hundred years apart provide intriguing glimpses into Seminole daily life during periods of time when the Seminoles were poorly known to the outside world. The first is William Bartram's *Travels*, published in 1791 and reprinted or annotated several times in recent years. Bartram's visits to Seminoles living near present-day Palatka on the St. Johns River, Cuscowilla near Paynes Prairie south of Gainesville, and Talahasochte on the Suwannee River are recounted with both poetic eloquence and keen observation. It is from Bartram that we learn what the log cabins of Cuscowilla looked like, how adulterers were punished, and what kinds of crops grew in Seminole fields.

The second firsthand account is the Reverend Clay MacCauley's 1884 report to the Smithsonian's J. W. Powell based on his visit to the Seminoles in the winter of 1880–1881. At Powell's request on behalf of Congress, MacCauley had been sent to Florida to find out how many Seminoles there were and how they were making a living. After more than twenty years of isolation following the Third Seminole War, the Seminoles had all but disappeared from view. Finally published by the Smithsonian's Bureau of Ethnology in 1887 (as pages 469–531 of their fifth annual report), *The Seminole Indians of Florida* brought the Seminoles to the attention of the outside world. MacCauley's sharp eye for rich cultural detail supplemented by numerous illustrations make this the first true anthropological study of the Seminoles.

The most comprehensive single source covering Seminole activities during the Second Seminole War (1835–1842) is John T. Sprague's *Origin, Progress, and Conclusion of the Florida War*, originally published in 1848 and reprinted by the University of Florida Press in 1964. Fighting first with the marines and then with the army infantry, Sprague experienced firsthand the conditions of war in Florida. His narrative is based on official military correspondence and documents but contains many references to the movements and leadership of the various Seminole bands.

The Indian Claims Commission hearings in 1957 regarding Seminole land claims resulted in two important modern studies of Seminole Indian culture and history. *The Ethnohistorical Report of the Florida Indians* by Charles H. Fairbanks, published by Garland in 1974, delves deeply into primary sources to reconstruct the origins and locations of the Seminoles prior to American possession of Florida and looks at the question, Did the Seminole nation as a distinct political entity exist during Spanish and British rule? John Goggin's study *Before the Indian Claims Commission*, published by the U.S. Government Printing Office in 1963, can be considered as a companion volume to the Fairbanks report. Goggin focuses on the concept of land tenure that prevailed under the Spanish administration.

The works of modern historians can be helpful in pointing the reader to specific primary sources. J. Leitch Wright's *Creeks and Seminoles* (University of Nebraska Press, 1986) and James W. Covington's *The Seminoles of Florida* (University Press of Florida, 1993) are well researched and extensively documented studies. Modern political developments involving the Seminole Tribe are detailed in *An Assumption of Sovereignty* by Harry A. Kersey, Jr., published in 1996 by the University of Nebraska Press.

Archaeological perspectives on Seminole culture history are provided in my 1989 book *Like Beads on a String*, published by the University of Alabama Press. The significance of the archaeological excavations of Seminole burials from the Fort Brooke cemetery in Tampa is discussed in "Cultural Responses to Stress: Patterns Observed in American Indian Burials of the Second Seminole War," by Harry M. Piper, Kenneth W. Hardin, and

Jacquelyn G. Piper in *Southeastern Archaeology* 1 (2) (1982): 122–37, and in the Pipers' 1982 report *Archaeological Excavations at the Quad Block Site, 8-Hi-998*.

Seminole Indian material culture is considered in Patricia Wickman's *Osceola's Legacy* (University of Alabama Press, 1991) and is the focus of *Art of the Florida Seminole and Miccosukee Indians* by Dorothy Downs (University Press of Florida, 1995) and *Patchwork and Palmettos* by David M. Blackard (Fort Lauderdale Historical Society, 1990). The *Florida Anthropologist*, the quarterly journal of the Florida Anthropological Society, consistently publishes articles on various aspects of Seminole history, culture, society, and archaeology. Over the years Wilfred T. Neill, Robert Carr, and Patsy West have contributed important pieces to this journal.

Taken together, these references will form a sturdy foundation for the reader hoping to build further understandings of the rich culture of Florida's Seminole and Miccosukee Indians.

TIMELINE

1997 Ah-Tah-Thi-Ki, "A Place to Remember," a 5,000-square-foot museum exhibiting the history and culture of the Seminole Tribe opens on the Big Cypress Reservation on August 23.

1990 $50 million Seminole Land Claims settlement divided 75/25 among the Oklahoma Seminoles and the Florida Seminoles, Miccosukees, and Independents by order of Congress.

1980 The remains of Seminole men, women, and children interred in the Fort Brooke cemetery during the Second Seminole War excavated by archaeologists under contract to the city of Tampa prior to the construction of a new municipal parking garage.

1970 Indian Claims Commission agrees to award $12 million in the Seminole land claims case but fails to specify the means of division between the Florida and Oklahoma tribes. An appeal by the Florida Seminoles resulted in a 1976 decision to award $16 million, still without a formula for division. By 1990 the claim would grow to $50 million.

1962 The Miccosukee Tribe of Indians gains federal recognition.

1957 The Seminole Tribe of Florida gains federal recognition.

1950 A small group of Seminoles files a land claims suit before the Indian Claims Commission seeking compensation for lands lost prior to the Second Seminole War and to Everglades National Park in 1935.

1939 Seminole village re-created at the New York World's Fair.

1928 Tamiami Trail (now U.S. 41) opens between Naples and Miami, crossing the Everglades and attracting settlements of Indians who later would form the Miccosukee Tribe.

1916–1918 Colorful patchwork style of clothing created by Seminole women using hand-cranked sewing machines. Early designs are "Fire" and "Rain."

1880–1881 The Reverend Clay MacCauley visits South Florida at the request of the U.S. government to evaluate the current living conditions of the Florida Seminoles.

c. 1867 Abiaka (Sam Jones), guiding spirit of the Seminole resistance against U.S. removal attempts through two wars, dies in South Florida.

1855–1858 Seminole resistance to the final armed attempt at their removal by the federal government results in the Third Seminole War. Billy Bowlegs and his band emigrate to Indian Territory, leaving no more than two hundred Seminoles in Florida.

1842 The Second Seminole War ends without a treaty. Almost 4,000 Seminoles were deported to Indian Territory, untold hundreds were killed in action or died awaiting deportation. Approximately three hundred Seminoles survive in Florida.

1838 Osceola, famed warrior who led the resistance in the early years of the Second Seminole War, dies in captivity at Fort Moultrie, South Carolina, on January 31.

1837 Indian warriors under Sam Jones, the Prophet, Halpatter Tustenuggee (Alligator), and Wildcat meet troops under the command of Zachary Taylor in the Battle of Okeechobee on Christmas Day.

1835 Seminole warriors ambush Major Francis Dade and his troops on the Fort King Road, signaling their intent not to leave Florida without a fight and beginning the Second Seminole War.

1823 The Treaty of Moultrie Creek expresses the government's Indian policy of containment of the Seminoles and their removal to Indian Territory.

1821 Florida is transferred from Spain to the United States. Andrew Jackson serves briefly as the first governor. A territorial government is established in 1822.

1818 General Andrew Jackson invades Spanish Florida to attack and destroy Seminole villages at Lake Miccosukee and the Suwannee River under orders to quell border tensions in what became known as the First Seminole War.

1813 King Payne, nephew of Cowkeeper and leader of the Alachua band of Seminoles, dies of wounds sustained in battle
with Colonel Daniel Newnan and the Georgia militia near
what is now Paynes Prairie.

1778 Joseph Purcell maps the mission road through North Florida
for British governor John Stuart, showing the locations of ten
Seminole towns in the panhandle and north peninsula.

1774 William Bartram, naturalist from Philadelphia, visits Cowkeeper's Cuscowilla village near the Alachua savanna, White
King's Talahasochte village on the Suwannee River, and
trading houses on the St. Johns. His *Travels*, published in
1791, brings international attention to the Florida Seminoles.

1765 In the Treaty of Picolata, a council of Creek Indians cedes
Florida east of the St. Johns River to the British. Cowkeeper
withholds participation in the council, beginning the political
separation of Creek and Seminole.

     The surveyor William DeBrahm maps Florida for the
British colonial government, using the term *Seminolskees* to
refer to the Indians he encountered.

1715 Emperor Brim of the Lower Creeks fails in an effort to
destroy the South Carolina colony in the Yamasee War, setting
the stage for Creek movement into Florida.

1702 British-backed Creek raids destroy the Spanish missions of
Florida.

1607–1702 Spanish missions proliferate in North Florida, changing
aboriginal settlement patterns in the lower Southeast.

1565 Pedro Menéndez de Avilés founds St. Augustine, establishing
the European colonial presence in the Southeast.

1528–1565 Expeditions of Spanish conquistadores penetrate Florida and
the interior, coming in contact with peoples ancestral to the
Creeks and Seminoles.

10,000 B.C. Aboriginal peoples inhabit the coastlines, wetlands, and river
–A.D. 1528 basins of what is now the southeastern United States. Gathering, fishing, and hunting lifeways predominate, with intensive harvesting of plants and shellfish allowing local population densities to develop. Corn farming in some areas
is associated with chiefdoms by A.D. 900. Many cultures
throughout the region use burial mounds for their dead and
construct flat-topped temple mounds for ceremonies.